Kentucky HANDICAP HORSE RACING

Kentucky HANDICAP HORSE RACING

A History of the Great Weight Carriers

MELANIE GREENE

THE History PRESS

Published by The History Press
Charleston, SC 29403
www.historypress.net

First published 2014

Manufactured in the United States

ISBN 978.1.62619.469.4

Library of Congress CIP data applied for.

Contents

FOREWORD

In her examination of the history of Kentucky-bred handicap horses, Melanie Greene has done a long overdue paean to those past champions that labored under seemingly impossible imposts and still managed to win consistently. By restricting her book to Kentucky-breds, she has had to omit such great handicap horses as Stymie, Gallorette and Dr. Fager, to name just a few. However, it would be a monumental task to discuss all the great weight carriers in Thoroughbred history while still keeping this book at a reasonable length. She has done a commendable job in picking the Kentucky-breds that have made the final cut.

As Ms. Greene points out, the handicap horses that consistently raced while carrying 130 pounds or more have vanished from the horse-racing scene. Today, there are so many lucrative stakes races for older horses that a trainer is able to pick and choose what race his or her champion will run in, and every racing secretary is aware that a race in which that trainer's horse would be required to carry 135 pounds would not be on the short list.

In concluding that the era of serious handicap racing is over, I have mixed feelings concerning its disappearance. No other sport punishes its most gifted participants because of his or her outstanding ability. One can marvel while watching the replay of the 1976 Marlboro Cup, in which Forego overcame his assigned weight of 137 pounds and a sloppy track that he despised to defeat that year's Travers winner, Honest Pleasure, who was carrying a feathery 119 pounds. However, it is with some sadness that one reads of the great Discovery finishing last in the 1936 Merchants' and Citizens' Handicap while carrying 143 pounds. The winner of that race, the gifted filly Esposa, was given a 43-pound weight advantage. (Two weeks later, in the weight-for-age Whitney, Discovery beat Esposa by ten lengths while conceding five pounds to that rival.) It should also be noted that racing fans were denied the privilege of watching the immortal Man o' War race as a four-year-old after his owner, Sam Riddle, was informed that his champion's normal impost would be 145 pounds.

So sit back and enjoy reading how the great weight carriers of their time did something that will never be seen again in racing history.

ALLAN CARTER, HISTORIAN
National Museum of Racing

PREFACE

Jesse Owens never had to race with ankle weights. Carl Lewis never gave anyone a head start. But in handicap racing, good Thoroughbreds are penalized. They must carry more weight than less talented opponents. Great Thoroughbreds carry significantly more weight; the better they are, the heavier the penalty.[1]

This book documents a once-celebrated type of horse race—the handicap—in which horses are assigned weights based on their past performances as a way to try to create evenly matched fields. The better the horse, the heavier the weight assigned. In the twentieth century, handicaps frequently determined champion honors, especially for older horses, and were a popular attraction for geldings, which, unlike colts, had no need to be hastily retired to stand at stud.

It was Kentucky-bred horses that won under the heaviest of weights, dominating the handicap division year after year. These equine stars brought recognition to the Sport of Kings and became renowned athletes for their courage, fortitude and durability. Despite the historical importance of handicap racing and the significant contributions made by the Kentucky breeding and racing industries, handicapping has become a forgotten chapter in racing history and, as yet, remains unrecorded in a comprehensive volume.

Today, the majority of stakes races, including those that were formerly designated as handicaps, are weight-for-age events, and horses are rarely asked to carry more than 126 pounds. Champion handicappers are no longer recognized in a separate awards division. The ability to win under heavy weight has become a lost art. This book focuses on the racing careers and feats of leading Kentucky-bred racehorses that were crowned champions in the handicap division based on their ability to win under heavy weight assignments.

Admittedly, it is not a complete study of racing's greatest handicappers, as it focuses entirely on male racehorses, excluding many fantastic fillies and mares that won under heavy weight assignments, as well as a great many more horses bred in other states or countries that set the racing world afire with new speed and weight records. Nonetheless, this book serves as a tribute to the handicap and profiles some of the greatest equine weight carriers of racing's past.

ACKNOWLEDGEMENTS

Cathy Schenck at Keeneland Library (Lexington, Kentucky), who provided invaluable resources and photographs.

Victoria Tokarowski, curator at the National Museum of Racing and Hall of Fame (Saratoga Springs, New York), for her hours spent researching, locating and scanning photographs.

Allan Carter, historian at the National Museum of Racing and Hall of Fame, for writing the foreword.

Heather Rohde for painting the beautiful portraits of the champions profiled in the book.

Linda Rainey at the Canadian Horse Racing Hall of Fame (Toronto, Ontario), who provided a photograph of Ted Atkinson and Tom Fool.

Lisa J. Hall at the Aiken Thoroughbred Racing Hall of Fame and Museum (Aiken, South Carolina) for providing a photo of Devil Diver.

The staff at Memorial University of Newfoundland's Digital Media Centre, who assisted with scanning and photo editing.

The staff at The History Press, especially my commissioning editor, Banks Smither.

Erika Steeves, for proofreading the manuscript and offering feedback and suggestions.

Chapter 1

HISTORY OF THE HANDICAP

The mark of a great horse is to carry weight over distances...Put in simple terms, a horse cannot be considered great until he has won—hopefully repeatedly at the classic distance of a mile and a quarter or more. And he cannot be considered great until he has carried more than scale weight, in practical terms 130 pounds or more, and given away chunks of weight to good competition.[2]

ORIGINS OF THE "HANDICAP"

"Hand-in-cap" was a lottery game dating back to the fourteenth century.[3] The game required three people—two players and a referee or matchmaker. All three placed forfeit money into a cap, with ownership determined by the outcome of the game. Each of the two players would offer up an item he thought the other would want. The referee assigned value to the items; the difference in value between the two items was referred to as the "boot" or "odds."[4]

The person who offered up the lesser-valued item had to pay up with the amount decreed by the referee. If in agreement with the swap, the players would then reach into the cap and draw out loose change. This change was symbolic and did not become part of the appraisal fee. If both players drew out coins, the exchange of items was carried out, and the referee took the forfeit money. If neither player drew out coins, the referee again took the forfeit money, and the exchange was not made. If only one player took out coins, he was entitled to the forfeit money, and no exchange was made.

Eventually, the name of the game was shortened to "hand i'cap" and then "handicap," and the word came to refer to any effort to make a contest more equitable. In horse racing, the equalization was carried out by placing weights under the saddle of the faster horse to bring its skill level or ability down to match the other starters of the race.

Handicaps in Thoroughbred Horse Racing

The system of handicap racing was designed to make races competitive and interesting, with a spread in weight designed to "level the playing field so the race was worth betting on."[5] It has been said that handicaps were once even "necessary" when racing secretaries relied on local heroes to fill races and assigning weight to these champions provided other trainers with an incentive to enter their horses in hopes of an upset.[6]

Owners and trainers considered heavy weight assignments to be an honor and were often willing to rise to the challenge. John Hay Whitney, co-owner of Greentree Stable, exclaimed before the 1953 Brooklyn, "Do you realize they put 136 pounds on Tom Fool for the Brooklyn Handicap? Isn't it wonderful that they think so much of my horse?"[7] Winning under imposts of more than 130 pounds was seen to raise the profile of young stallions. Handicaps once accounted for the majority of stakes races and were known to boast some of the biggest purses, attracting the leading horses of the day.

But things didn't start off that way. The handicap started as a betting-appeal race on British racetracks in the 1800s. Admiral Henry John Rous, who introduced the weight-for-age scale, wrote in the mid-nineteenth century, "A handicap is intended to encourage bad horses and to put them on a par with the best. It is a racing lottery—a vehicle for gambling on an extensive scale, producing the largest field of horses at the smallest expense."[8]

According to an article written by Sir Henry de Gelsey entitled "The Handicap" and published in the June 1953 issue of *The British Racehorse*, the earliest handicap that was ever run in England was the Subscription Handicap Plate, run over the Rowley Mile at Newmarket and open to all ages.[9] The first winner of the race, in 1785, was a six-year-old bay mare that carried a top weight of 136 pounds. The handicap race as it is now known did not become an important event on the racing calendar in England until 1839, when the Cesarewitch and the Cambridgeshire were inaugurated.[10]

The Cesarewitch, open to horses three years of age and older, is held at Newmarket in October and is run at a distance of two miles and two furlongs. The race is named for Tsesarevich Alexander, later Tsar Alexander II, who donated 300 pounds to The Jockey Club. The Cambridgeshire is held at Newmarket over a distance of one mile and one furlong and takes place in late September. The two races are referred to as the Autumn Double, and three horses were victorious in both races in the nineteenth century: Rosebery, Foxhall and Plaisanterie.

The Great Metropolitan Handicap and the City and Suburban Handicap were two of the first most prestigious handicaps to be run in the United Kingdom, first hosted at Epsom Racetrack in 1846 and 1851, respectively. The former, one of the first races to be sponsored, was born from efforts to boost the spring racing meet with support from local businesses. Up until 1985, it was contested over a grueling two and a quarter miles over an unusual course that was run in the reverse direction for three furlongs before turning right to rejoin the Derby course about a mile from the finish. It has now been reduced to a distance of a mile and a half and is run over the Derby course.

The City and Suburban once attracted top-quality horses; particularly noteworthy was the filly Virago, who won both this event and the Great Metropolitan, as well as two other prep races in April 1854 en route to a victory in the 1,000 Guineas in May. Today, the mile-and-a-quarter race is open to horses four years of age and older and is considered a less prestigious event.[11]

The oldest North American horse race was originally staged as a handicap. Now known as the Phoenix Stakes, the Phoenix Hotel Handicap was first run in 1831 at the Keeneland Association Racetrack in Lexington, Kentucky, where it was staged until 1930. The race got its name from the local Phoenix Hotel. Not run between 1931 and 1936, the Phoenix was restarted at Keeneland Racecourse in 1937. Now a part of the Breeders Cup Challenge series, the Phoenix is a qualifier for the Breeders Cup Sprint. In 2014, the Phoenix will be in its 162nd running. It is a six-furlong race on the dirt for three-year-olds and up, and weights are assigned.

Colonel M. Lewis Clark Jr., founder of the Louisville Jockey Club and builder of Churchill Downs, inaugurated the Clark Handicap in 1875. Until 1901, it was run at the Downs as a stakes race open to three-year-old colts and fillies over a distance of two miles. Today, it is open to horses aged three years and up and is run over a distance of a mile and one eighth, with weights assigned.

Clark also established several other handicaps at the Downs, including the Falls City Handicap for fillies and mares aged three and up and the Louisville Cup. The latter was a handicap for older horses and was first run in 1875, three days after the inaugural Kentucky Derby. The crowd of spectators that showed up for the Cup exceeded that which turned out for the Derby by several thousand, and the *Daily Graphic* reported that "not only the citizens, but the entire State seems to have turned out in force."[12] Yet it would be the Derby that later rose to prominence, while the Cup was discontinued after 1887.[13]

Today, the Louisville Handicap, introduced in 1895, is raced on turf, open to horses aged three years and up and run in late May over a distance of a mile and a half. Two horses have won the race three times (and also consecutively): Chorwon and Silverfoot.

A Kentucky-bred horse of early handicap fame was the stallion Ten Broeck, named for Richard Ten Broeck, a well-known horseman and owner of notable sire Lexington. In 1875, Ten Broeck won the Phoenix Hotel Handicap, in which he defeated eventual Derby winner Aristides, but faded to fifth in the Derby. The bay won a total of five races in nine starts as a three-year-old and returned to the track at four to take the Louisville Cup (as well as six other races) and set a new world-record time for a four-mile walkover on dirt. He continued to race at ages five and six, and in his final season, he won a match race in Louisville against the California mare Molly McCarthy. The race is recounted in the lyrics of a Kentucky folk song, "Molly and Tenbrooks." Ten Broeck was inducted into the National Museum of Racing and Hall of Fame in 1982.

While the state of Kentucky is recognized as the first to hold handicaps, tracks in New York and California later emerged to host the most prestigious of these races. The Suburban and Metropolitan Handicaps, modeled after their British counterparts, were first run in 1884 and 1891, respectively. According to Irene McCanliss in *Weight on the Thoroughbred Racehorse*, the Suburban was the first true, present-day type of handicap of any importance. Established by Walter S. Vosburgh at Sheepshead Bay, it was run at a mile and a quarter and open to horses three years of age and older. It quickly became the "most talked-of race in the country."[14]

In 1915, the Suburban was transferred to Empire City Race Track, after which it moved to Belmont Park, where it continues to be held each July. From 1961 to 1974, as well as in 1976, it was held at Aqueduct. In 1975, it was contested at a distance of a mile and a half and at a mile and three-sixteenths the following year. Today, it is run at a mile and one-eighth. Five horses have won this event on two occasions: Crusader, Kelso, Winter's Tale, Devil His Due and Flat Out.

The Metropolitan Handicap, known as the "Met Mile," was first held at Morris Park Racecourse in the Bronx at a distance of a mile and one-eighth. In 1897, it was changed to its current distance of one mile. In 1904, it moved to its current location of Belmont Park, where it has been held since with the exception of the years 1960–67, 1969 and 1975, when it was hosted by Aqueduct Racetrack. Devil Diver holds the record for most wins with three. Equipoise also won it three times but was disqualified in 1934. The race is held during the last week of May.

The Brooklyn Handicap, inaugurated at Gravesend in 1887, became the second leg of what is referred to as the New York Handicap Triple series of races, run in between the Metropolitan and Suburban in early June, initially at a distance of a mile and a quarter. Over the years, it has been run at distances ranging from one mile to its current distance of a mile and a half and at various New York tracks, including Belmont Park, where it was hosted in 1957, 1975 and from 1977 to the present.[15] Discovery and Forego were both victorious in the Brooklyn on three occasions. Today, it is a weight-for-age event, a type of race in which all horses carry weight according to the official scale of weights, which sets assignments based on age and sex, regardless of past performance.

All three of the Handicap Triple races were created as highweight handicaps. Only four horses have won all three races in the same year: Whisk Broom II, Tom Fool, Kelso and Fit to Fight.

The Manhattan Handicap has historically been a premier event for top racehorses. Open to three-year-olds and up, the race has been run at various distances (but today is run at a distance of a mile and a quarter) and has been hosted at Belmont Park since 1905. Originally run on the dirt course, it was moved to the turf course in 1970.[16] Interestingly, the year of its inauguration is somewhat unclear. Beginning in 1867, a race identical to the Manhattan was run at Jerome Park (and between 1887 and 1896 at Morris Park Racetrack in the Bronx) but was not identified as such until 1872. However, the New York Racing Association and the American Racing Manual have its start date recorded as 1896. Previously held in the fall meet, the Manhattan is now held the first Saturday in June on the Belmont Stakes undercard.

The Jerome Handicap was first run in 1866 as the Jerome Stakes. From 1867 to 1872, it was run as the Champion Stakes, and it did not become a handicap until 1893. Until 1899, it was hosted by Jerome Park, after which time it was moved to Morris Park, where it was held until 1905. From 1906 to the present, it has been run at Belmont Park in January. While it has been run at various distances over the years, today it is run at a distance of one mile and seventy yards and is open only to three-year-olds, with weight assigned.

The Carter Handicap is a seven-furlong race open to three-year-olds and up and run each April at Aqueduct. Inaugurated in 1895, the Carter is renowned for being the only North American horse race in which a triple dead heat occurred for the win (1944). The winners were Brownie, Bossuet and Wait a Bit. Bossuet carried 127 pounds, conceding 12 pounds to Brownie and 9 pounds to Wait a Bit. Top weight of 132 pounds went to Apache, who finished farther back in the field.

Saratoga once played host to several premier handicaps that are now defunct. The Merchants' and Citizens' Handicap, inaugurated in 1901, was discontinued after 1954. The race was open to horses three years of age and older and contested over various distances over its fifty-three-year span. Sir Barton set a world record for the race at a mile and three-sixteenths in 1920. The Saratoga Handicap, also first run in 1901, was contested over a mile and a quarter. A son of leading sire Lexington named Kentucky won the first two runnings of the race. Champion handicapper Exterminator won an unprecedented four editions between 1919 and 1922. The event was discontinued after 1961.

The Santa Anita Handicap, first run in 1935 at the California track after which it is named, is one of the few original handicaps that is still run as such, with weights assigned based on the previous performances of the horses entered in the race. It also has one of the largest purses in the handicap division, offering $750,000 in the 2013 edition. Such champions as Seabiscuit, Noor, Affirmed, Spectacular Bid and John Henry have won the race.

Prior to 1971, annual "Champion Handicap Male Horse" honors were awarded to horses three years of age and older, with winners chosen first by the *Daily Racing Form* and the *Turf and Sports Digest* beginning in 1936. Then, in 1950, the Thoroughbred Racing Association (TRA) began naming its own champion. Champions between 1874 and 1935 were determined retrospectively by a panel of experts and published by *Blood-Horse* magazine. In 1971, the award became part of the Eclipse Awards program. The title was changed, as was the award criteria, making only horses four years of age or older eligible for "American Champion Older Male Horse" honors. A full list of the twentieth- and twenty-first-century winners of these awards to date can be found in Appendices A and B.

Chapter 2

ROSEBEN: THE BIG TRAIN

Roseben was known as the greatest sprinter of his time and the first real great weight carrier of the twentieth century. He was nicknamed the "Big Train" not only for his size but also for his ability to carry heavy weights over short distances. Roseben often competed in "overnighters"—races in which the weight was set the day before and, on the day of the race, the horse's connections could either accept the weight or scratch. He ran and won with as much as 147 pounds on numerous occasions, setting or equaling track records at distances of six, seven and seven and a half furlongs. The most weight he ever carried was 150 pounds, in a handicap at Gravesend in 1906, and on this occasion he ran second, losing by a length and a half to Comedienne, to whom he conceded 58 pounds.[17]

Bred by Thomas J. Carson of Lexington, Kentucky's Dixiana Stud, the bay was sired by the Bend Or stud Ben Strome, leading sire in 1903, and out of the mare Rose Leaf (Duke of Montrose). Foaled in 1901, Roseben was slow to mature but eventually grew to an enormous size, measuring just one inch shy of eighteen hands. Sold as a yearling, already gelded, to John Drake, he was initially conditioned by Enoch Wishard and raced only once as a two-year-old and lost, finishing tenth in a four-and-a-half-furlong allowance race at Nashville.[18]

At three, Roseben was unplaced in two starts in New York. In his first race, he carried 98 pounds and finished fifth. He finally broke his maiden in a six-and-a-half-furlong maiden race in October at Morris Park in the Bronx. On a sloppy track, and while carrying 107 pounds, the gelding won easily by two

Roseben. *Courtesy of the National Museum of Racing and Hall of Fame.*

lengths.[19] He was swiftly auctioned off to Davy Johnson for $3,800. Trained by Charlie Oxx, he went on to win two overnighters for a total of three wins in nine starts that season.

As a four-year-old, Roseben began to hit his stride, racing through the winter in Arkansas and Washington and then moving in April to Aqueduct, where he finished second in the Carter Handicap.[20] Roseben arrived at the brand-new Belmont Park for the six-furlong Toboggan Handicap to contest the colt Race King, who had dead-heated with Sysonby two days prior in the Metropolitan Handicap. Carrying 2 pounds more than the favorite, Roseben easily defeated his new rival. Unplaced in the Crotona Handicap, Roseben returned in the Claremont for a rematch with Race King, to whom he conceded 9 pounds and ran away laughing. Assigned 140 pounds, the big gelding won his next time out, followed by a third-place performance and then placing in the Coney Island Handicap.

Under the direction of new trainer Frank D. Weir, Roseben next claimed five consecutive overnighters before finishing sixth in the one-mile Delaware Handicap,[21] defeated by the filly Molly Brant, who finished first under 113 pounds, and champion mare Beldame, who ran fifth under 122 pounds (the same weight he carried).[22] Roseben followed this up with a victory at six furlongs under 140 pounds and two second-place finishes and then proceeded to win a string of New York handicaps. In the Bronx Highweight, he carried 140 pounds. Two days later, Roseben carried 147 pounds in the Manhattan, winning by five lengths and giving 42 pounds to his nearest rival, Aeronaut, and 43 pounds to third-place finisher Race King.[23] In the process, he set two records: a new American record, running 1:11⅗ for six furlongs, and a new American weight-carrying record. Four days later, he returned to Belmont Park to set a seven-furlong record at 1:25⅕ under 126 pounds. At year's end, he had won eleven races in twenty starts.

In 1906, at five years of age, Roseben started in twenty-two races, winning eleven, placing in five and running third in three.[24] He won the richest race of his career, the $7,850 Carter Handicap, in which he conceded 23 pounds to the runner-up, Southern Cross. In the Sterling Stakes, Roseben won for the first time in his career at a mile, defeating Ram's Horn and carrying 127 pounds. His time for the race was 1:40⅕.[25] Tried at longer distances, however, Roseben could do no better than fifth in the mile-and-one-sixteenth Excelsior Handicap and seventh in the mile-and-one-quarter Brooklyn Handicap. In between these two races, he set a new track record at Belmont Park of 1:32⅕ for seven and a half furlongs.

Two days after a victory in the Flight Stakes, the gelding started in a six-furlong overnight handicap carrying 144 pounds. At odds of 1–3, he gave 44

Roseben, 1906. *Courtesy of the author.*

pounds to the filly Suffrage and sprinted home by three-quarters of a length. Four days later, Roseben was assigned 150 pounds in the Fall Handicap and lost to Comedienne, who caught him in the stretch and won by two lengths.[26]

On September 1, Roseben raced at Sheepshead Bay, carrying 132 pounds over six furlongs. He won in 1:12⅖ by two lengths, defeating Neva Lee and Ormondale. Seventeen days later, he carried 144 pounds to victory over six furlongs in 1:12⅗.[27] On October 12, Roseben won the Manhattan for a second time, again carrying 147 pounds and conceding 36 pounds to the second horse, Suffrage, who carried 111 pounds.[28] He won by six lengths, and his time for the six furlongs was 1:12⅕.[29] He closed out the season with six stakes wins and earnings totaling $27,870, the highest of his career.[30]

On October 16, Roseben set a new American record (1:22) for seven furlongs, winning an allowance race at Belmont Park under 126 pounds, in which he contested only one rival, the Salvator colt Beauclere, who carried 85 pounds.[31] It would be forty years before the record was beaten at Hollywood Park by the great race mare Honeymoon and fifty years before Bold Ruler beat it at Belmont. [32] The *Daily Racing Form* reported on Roseben's performance:

> *Roseben, the champion sprinter of the year, and the fastest horse of his time, ran 7 furlongs around one turn in 1:22. There were 15,000 people at the course (Belmont Park) and they nearly cheered themselves hoarse at this most wonderful achievement on the part of Davy Johnson's breadwinner. The best previous record for the seven-eighths of a mile was 1:23½, made by Bella B. over the straightaway at Monmouth Park. The previous record for this course was 1:25 flat. Roseben returned to the scales as the band played "Hail to the Chief."*[33]

Two weeks later, Roseben was asked to carry 148 pounds in the six-furlong Richmond Handicap. Bumped by Jacobite in the stretch, he faded to finish third by one and a half lengths. Jacobite was disqualified, and Roseben was moved up to second place behind Oxford, who placed first.[34]

In 1907, as a six-year-old, Roseben raced in the Carter Handicap for the third time, this time carrying 135 pounds and conceding 13 pounds to Water Light and Oxford.[35] Starting as the favorite,[36] he finished second behind Glorified, who carried 119 pounds. He rebounded to capture a six-furlong handicap at Brighton Beach in mid-July by two lengths, conceding 60 pounds to the runner-up, Smoker. Roseben finished third in both the Metropolitan and Equality Stakes. Shortly after his second victory in the

Flight Stakes—his seventh win of fourteen starts that season—the *New York Times* reported that the champion sprinter was dying of blood poisoning, supposedly the result of having stepped on a sharp stone.[37]

Roseben survived this ordeal and continued to race at age seven, wining nine of twenty-six races, twice carrying 140 pounds and finishing third in the Claremont Handicap and Bayshore Selling Stakes. That fall, he was shipped from New York to California and won three overnight races at Oakland.[38] The Big Train gradually began to lose steam, and at eight he won only three races in ten starts, earning $2,415. Roseben eventually wound up in the claiming ranks. In his last start, he bowed a tendon, finishing the race in second place.

In 111 starts, Roseben won 52 times and retired with career earnings of $75,110.[39] According to the National Museum of Racing and Hall of Fame, in 86 races, Roseben gave weight to all of his rivals and won 14 races carrying 140 pounds or more (he raced 29 times carrying such a burden). Four times he carried 148 pounds, accruing three seconds and a third-place finish.

After his retirement, Roseben was gifted to New York congressman James Wadsworth, who gave the horse to his daughter, Mrs. Fletcher Harper, as a pleasure horse. The *Thoroughbred Record* announced in April 1911 that the young woman never had a problem handling the big horse, claiming he was "as gentle as a kitten."[40] Roseben died in 1918 at age seventeen. He was inducted into the Hall of Fame in 1956. The Roseben Handicap was run in his honor at Belmont Park from 1940 until 1995 (and at Aqueduct from 1962 to 1982). It was a six-furlong event open to horses three years of age and older and, at the time of its cancellation, was a Grade II race.

Chapter 3

Roamer: The Accidental Champion

The truly great racehorse appears infrequently. At least one such graced the racing of 1914. Andrew Miller's Roamer displayed all the qualities that appear in the makeup of a star of the first magnitude: Amazing speed, as well as the ability to carry high weight and stay over any route were demonstrated publicly time and again.[41]

Roamer was an accident. As the offspring of a "teaser" stallion and a blind claiming mare, his owners had little expectations for him. The bay gelding put his doubters to shame, winning under burdens of up to 133 pounds, and broke more track records than any other racehorse of his era. He raced and won at varying distances for seven years, started a total of ninety-eight times, captured the Saratoga Handicap three times and was inducted into the Hall of Fame in 1981. He just made the list of Blood-Horse's *Top 100 Racehorses of the 20th Century*, ranked at number ninety-nine.

In 1910, Colonel E.F. Clay was the chairman of the Kentucky State Racing Commission and was in partnership with his brother-in-law, Colonel Catesby Woodford, as co-owner of Runnymede Stud near Paris, Kentucky. The two men were considering breeding the mare Rose Tree II, a daughter of Bona Vista, to Star Shoot, an American import who would eventually lead the North American sire list five times and father such champions as Triple Crown winner Sir Barton and handicapper Grey Lag. At fourteen years of age, Rose Tree II was no spring chicken and had been claimed in England for a meager £200. Furthermore, she was blind.

The story goes that Clay was reluctant to send her to the stallion Star Shoot, as he was also blind. The problem was solved (although a new one quickly arose) when the mare was found to be in foal to the stud farm's teaser stallion, Knight Errant. It is not clear which horse jumped the fence, but one of them did, and so Roamer came to be.

Despite his previous lack of success as a stud (and thus his delegation to teaser stallion duties), Knight Errant came from decent bloodlines. Out of the Australian stallion Trenton, himself a son of Ascot winner and good sire Musket, he was out of a St. Simon mare. Interestingly, Roamer's half sister Rosewood, out of the stallion Magneto, would go on to produce three stakes winners.

Unplanned from the start, Roamer surprised his owners and spectators alike when he won at first asking, capturing a four-and-a-half-furlong maiden race in Lexington by five lengths on May 1, 1913. He lost his next four starts, although in the latter two, Old Rosebud, a grandson of Star Shoot (and the next year's Derby winner), defeated him. On May 17, in a four-and-a-half-furlong allowance race for two-year-olds at Churchill Downs, Roamer ran in second place from start to finish behind the bay gelding. And on June 4, he finished third behind him and Little Nephew in an allowance at Douglas Park. Old Rosebud would go on to retrospectively receive Champion Two-Year-Old honors for that year. Meanwhile, Roamer rebounded from those defeats to take an overnighter by six lengths at Latonia.

Perhaps looking to make a quick profit off the unwanted gelding, Clay entered Roamer in a $1,000, five-and-a-half-furlong claiming race at Belmont Park. The bay led wire to wire and took the win by four lengths. The winning purse amounted to only $380, and perhaps reconsidering the potential value of the horse, Clay had to put up $2,005 to outbid Albert Simons's $2,000. A few days later, however, Jack Goldsborough, trainer for Andrew Miller, offered $2,500 for Roamer, which Clay accepted.

Born in Hamilton, Ontario, Miller was a Harvard graduate and a former classmate of Teddy Roosevelt. Miller founded the now-defunct magazine *Life*, was one of the first stewards of The Jockey Club and was among a group of influential horsemen, including W.C. Whitney, who purchased Saratoga Racetrack in 1900.

Racing in Miller's cardinal silks, white sash and black cap, Roamer managed a second-place finish behind Little Nephew in a handicap at Saratoga, his first start for his new owner. He came back in the Saratoga Special to defeat Black Toney. What followed was a seven-part series of puzzling and disappointing performances.

Roamer with McTaggart up. *Wikipedia.*

Roamer winning the Saratoga Special on August 9, 1913. *Courtesy of Keeneland-Cook.*

Roamer, Merritt Buxton up, Carter Handicap, 1914. *Courtesy of Keeneland-Cook.*

At age three, Roamer rose to prominence in the racing world as he demonstrated his ability to win with speed under heavy weight assignments and at varying distances. In 1914, he started sixteen times, won twelve and set five track records. He was the leading money earner of the year, with $29,105.[42] In his first start of the season, a six-furlong overnighter, the bay gelding won by four lengths while carrying 104 pounds. He next finished third, carrying 115 pounds, in the mile Withers Stakes, defeated by long-shot Charlestonian. Old Rosebud pulled up lame. Running against older horses for the first time in the Toboggan, Roamer finished a dismal fourteenth. He bounced back to win an overnighter by three lengths.

In the Carter Handicap, Roamer was assigned 109 pounds. He showed he could beat older horses as he "cantered home by two lengths,"[43] shattering Aqueduct's seven-furlong record by 1⅕ seconds in the process and returning home in 1:24⅘. Four days later, he ran the same distance just a fifth of a second off his own record.

Staying true to form, Roamer won the Brooklyn Derby (now the Dwyer Stakes) by eight lengths in a time of 2:05⅗, a new Aqueduct record for the distance. He lost his next start, the Empire City Handicap, to Buckhorn but went on to win his next six. He won the mile-and-a-half Midsummer Stakes by three lengths from Robert Oliver; the mile-and-a-quarter Travers by ten lengths, in which he set a Saratoga track record of 2:04; the Huron Handicap under 128 pounds; the State Fair Stakes, in which he defeated Gainer by eight lengths and set a new track record, breaking his own record for a mile-and-a-quarter of 2:02; the Municipal Handicap at Belmont Park; and the Autumn Weight-for-Age Stakes in a walk-over.

Two weeks later, Roamer, carrying 123 pounds, lost to Stromboli in the Baltimore Handicap at Laurel. He returned in the Washington Handicap to smash another track record and enact his revenge on his rival. Carrying 124 pounds, he won the mile-and-one-eighth race in 1:49⅗—an American record—under a hand ride. The *American Racing Manual* reported, "There has never been in this country such a remarkable exhibition of speed of the highest order as he gave at Laurel in the Washington Handicap."[44]

Roamer opened his four-year-old season with a win in a one-mile allowance race at Churchill Downs. After two losses in the Kentucky and Brooklyn Handicaps, he returned to the winner's circle in capturing the Queen's County Handicap over his old rival Stromboli. Next up came a puzzling performance in the Carter, in which he carried 130 pounds and didn't challenge at any point. This was followed by another victory just five days later in which he equaled Aqueduct's track record over Stromboli, to whom he conceded 4 pounds, in the mile-and-one-eighth Brookdale Handicap.

Continuing on to Belmont, Roamer was unplaced in the Empire City Handicap and then started four times in the month of August at Saratoga, winning three: the Saratoga Handicap, which he won by ten lengths; the Merchants' and Citizens' Handicap; and the Saratoga Cup. He lost the Champlain Handicap, in which he was burdened with 132 pounds, to Star Jasmine. Roamer closed out the season with wins in the Havre de Grace and the National Handicaps, defeating Stromboli both times. At year's end, Roamer was voted unofficial Champion Handicap male.

Roamer's first start in 1916 came on May 20. He carried 133 pounds in the King's County Handicap and couldn't make it on the board. He would suffer four more defeats before taking the mile-and-one-eighth Yonkers Handicap over Spur and Ed Crump, carrying 127 pounds. It would be his only win in thirteen starts as a five-year-old. Nonetheless, Roamer was voted Co-Champion Handicap male with Short Grass.

In 1917, Old Rosebud and Roamer met again for their six-year-old campaigns. On May 12, in an allowance race at Churchill Downs, Roamer "won easing up,"[45] with Ed Crump in second and Old Rosebud back in third. The gelding met with defeat in the Clark Handicap; after stumbling at the start, he finished behind Old Rosebud at the wire. In the Brooklyn, he was unplaced behind Borrow (whom he had defeated just a week prior in the Excelsior), the filly Regret and Old Rosebud. The latter would get the best of him in two other races that year: the Queens County and Delaware Handicaps. In the Queens County, Roamer, carrying 129 pounds, gave the Derby winner 4 pounds and finished in second place. In the Delaware, Old Rosebud was burdened with 133 pounds, and Roamer, carrying 127 pounds, finished third behind Capra. Roamer's five other wins that season (in a total of seventeen starts) came in the Saratoga Handicap, two overnights at Aqueduct, a handicap at Laurel Park and the Arlington Handicap.

As a seven-year-old, Roamer won his second Queen's County Handicap in four tries (123); his first Empire City Handicap in five tries (128); his first Mount Vernon in three tries, carrying 133 pounds; and his third consecutive Saratoga Handicap. In the latter, he was said to have shown "dazzling speed" in "galloping home three lengths in front"[46] despite carrying 129 pounds. Amazingly, he covered the mile-and-a-quarter race in 2:02⅕, breaking his own record set in the Travers four years before.

On August 21,1918, Roamer ran a mile under 110 pounds for the Saratoga Special in a race against time and shattered Salvator's record of 1:35½, which had stood for twenty-eight years.[47] A pacesetter, a two-year-old named Lightning, was used to trick Roamer into thinking it was a race and not a workout. In front of a crowd of two thousand, Roamer came home in a time of 1:34⅘.[48] His final win of the year came in the mile-and-one-eighth Pierrepont Handicap at Jamaica Racecourse on October 5, in which he carried 127 pounds and defeated Manister Toi and War Cloud. In sixteen starts, he was unplaced only twice.

In his final season, Roamer started six times and could manage only one win, a six-furlong handicap at Aqueduct in which he floated home under a feather-light 114 pounds to defeat Sun Briar. In his final race, the Yonkers Handicap, Roamer finished second behind Bally. Old Rosebud finished last.

Over a seven-year career, Roamer won at distances ranging from four and a half furlongs to one mile and three quarters, set or equaled eleven track records, won twenty-four stakes races and was twice named champion handicapper. He retired with career earnings of $98,828.[49] Goldsborough, who would go on to train Triple Crown winner Gallant

Fox, later commented, "In my opinion, there were only two great horses—Man o' War and Roamer."[50]

On December 31, 1919, Andrew Miller died at home from a heart attack. In a strange twist of fate, Roamer fractured his leg when he slipped in his paddock the next morning and was euthanized. Goldsborough once remarked of the gelding, "I never expect to see another like him."[51] The Roamer Handicap, originally contested at Jamaica Racecourse, was shifted to Aqueduct in 1959 and discontinued after 1987.

Chapter 4

Exterminator: Old Bones

Old Bones' courageous heart and iron body made him a legend. Perhaps his blood was not the bluest, nor his beginnings the most illustrious, but Exterminator was the epitome of the noble steed called the Thoroughbred, the exquisite blend of speed and stamina, the essence of class.[52]

Exterminator was best known for his longevity as a racehorse, competing until the age of nine. He got better as he got older; as a six-year-old, he set a track record in the two-mile Autumn Gold Cup, and at seven he defeated Grey Lag in the Brooklyn Handicap, carrying 135 pounds. He won the Pimlico Cup Handicap three times, the Saratoga Cup four times and carried imposts as heavy as 138 pounds to victory. Exterminator was inducted into the Hall of Fame in 1957. He is ranked number twenty-nine in Blood-Horse's *Top 100 Racehorses of the 20th Century*. In the words of his biographer, Eva Jolene Boyd, he "accomplish[ed] feats as a stayer and weight carrier that have never been equaled."[53]

Exterminator won stakes races at distances ranging from six furlongs to two and a quarter miles, competed at nineteen different racetracks in North America, had eight different trainers and was ridden by eighteen different jockeys throughout his career. He "established durability standards that rarely have been approached."[54] In ninety-nine "official starts," he holds the record for thirty-three stakes wins, set or equaled eight track records and earned a total of $252,996 over the course of his eight-year racing career.

Bred by F.D. "Dixie" Knight, Exterminator was foaled amid the turmoil of World War I on May 30, 1915, at Almahurst Farm in Jessamine County, near Nicholasville, Kentucky. He was sired by the English-bred stallion McGee, who was an unknown at the time but would later become the leading sire in America in 1922 after siring Donerail, the 1913 Kentucky Derby winner and the biggest long shot in Derby history at 99–1. His dam was Fair Empress, whose sire, Jim Gore, was second in the 1884 Derby behind Buchanan, whose own sire was Derby winner and Hall of Famer Hindoo.

Exterminator was sold as a yearling for $1,500 at Saratoga to J. Calvin Milam, who recalled, "He was right good looking…and he was well bred and I got him at what I considered a cheap price."[55] Milam's wife chose the name Exterminator when her husband asked her to suggest a name for a runner that he predicted would "vanquish his opponents."[56] The colt was sent to the Keeneland Association track for training under Albert Johnson, where he grew quickly to a height of 16.3hh. However, since he was slow to fill out, his new owner chose to have him gelded. It has also been speculated that he had a fiery disposition and was castrated in hopes of calming him down—further speculation points to his less-than-regal breeding.

The chestnut giant raced only four times as a two-year-old, and he won two of them. His debut came in a six-furlong maiden race at Latonia on June 30, 1917, which he won by three lengths over Mistress Polly and Quito. After finishing fourth in an allowance race in Windsor, Ontario, Canada, he returned three days later to win a five-and-a-half-furlong event at the same track. He ran once more, at Kenilworth Park, and ran last at the same distance. He came out of the race with a muscle sprain and was given the rest of the year off to grow into himself. Nonetheless, he earned back his purchase price in winner's purses and was nominated to the Derby.

Before the start of his three-year-old season, Exterminator was sold to Willis Sharpe Kilmer in exchange for $9,000 and two fillies.[57] Kilmer had purchased him as a workhorse for his star Derby prospect, Sun Briar, who had been purchased for $5,000 as a yearling at the same sale Exterminator in which had been sold.

Kilmer inherited a family fortune that was acquired from the sales of a medical concoction known as Swamp Root. He dropped out of Cornell University to manage the advertising for Kilmer and Company.[58] From his father he also inherited a love of horses. In 1915, he turned his attention from Standardbreds and show-jumpers to the establishment of a stud farm in Binghamton, New York.

Sun Briar was crowned Champion Two-Year-Old after securing five wins in nine starts; among his victories were the Saratoga Special, Grand Union Stakes and the Hopeful. He lugged 130 pounds in the last two, a high weight assignment for a juvenile. His earnings of $58,505 were the highest amassed by any horse that year. Needless to say, Kilmer, as well as racegoers, had great expectations for the colt in his three-year-old season. To the view of some, Kilmer went a little over the top with his parties held in honor of the horse. A welcome-home parade was hosted at the conclusion of his two-year-old season, and a birthday party was held in Binghamton on January 1 to celebrate Sun Briar's turning three, referred to in the press as the social event of the year.

As Sun Briar began preparing for his spring campaign, however, it became clear that the colt was not in top form. Arriving at Churchill Downs in mid-March, Kilmer's "golden boy" put in several good works but then bolted one day during a workout; it was speculated that he was hurting from ringbone. Meanwhile, Exterminator was catching some attention with his lightning-fast times in training. In late April, Sun Briar could only manage a third-place finish in a six-furlong prep race. Enter Exterminator.

Hoping that running the chestnut gelding alongside would help coax Sun Briar back into racing form, Kilmer refused to give up hope. Yet those hopes quickly faded. Records show that in their first workout together, Exterminator beat Sun Briar handily. At a longer distance their next time out, the tables were turned, with Sun Briar getting up to beat his new workmate. In their third and final workout, the colts were joined by stablemate Nelsweep. A large crowd turned out to witness Sun Briar try to beat War Cloud's record for ten furlongs, 2:01⅕, set the day before. The bay labored home in a final time of 2:12⅘ and was subsequently scratched from the Derby.

Most assumed at this point that Kilmer had bought Exterminator as a second Derby prospect. Frustrated, he issued a statement to the press denying any such intention: "In view of certain misleading press reports regarding my purchase of Exterminator, I desire to say that I did not acquire this horse as a Derby candidate, but as a trial horse…it is also well understood that I do not consider Exterminator in the same class with Sun Briar."[59]

The day before the Derby, Kilmer angrily retorted to Colonel Matt Winn, president of Churchill Downs, who inquired about Exterminator, "That horse isn't fast enough to run past me!"[60] Winn eventually convinced his friend to run him. Having not yet raced at three and dismissed at odds of 30–1, the lanky gelding came from behind to win by a length over seven other starters on a muddy track before a crowd of thirty thousand. Jockey Willie

Knapp later said of his mount, "When he was at his best, Exterminator could have beaten Man o' War or Citation or Kelso or any other horse that ever lived on any track doing anything."[61]

Exterminator went on to win six of fourteen more starts after the Derby as a three-year-old. After three second-place finishes under increasingly heavier weight assignments, he placed fourth in the Travers in August, defeated by Sun Briar. Following a trio of victories in five starts at Laurel Park, he won the Pimlico Autumn Handicap and then ran third in the Bowie Handicap. Against older horses, he won the two-miles-and-a-quarter Latonia Cup and then closed out the season five days later with a win in a mile-and-a-sixteenth handicap under 126 pounds.

In 1919, Exterminator started twenty-one times, winning nine races ranging from six to eighteen furlongs. In the Saratoga Cup, he equaled the track record of 2:58 for a mile and three-quarters despite a heavy downpour that resulted in a muddy track and saw attendance down on the track's closing day of the season. A crowd of nearly twenty thousand turned up to see up-and-coming two-year-old Man o' War win the Hopeful with "ridiculous ease" just prior to the running of the Cup.[62] In November, Exterminator won the inaugural Pimlico Cup at two and a quarter miles by four lengths. Sun Briar beat him once, in the Champlain Handicap.

After the conclusion of the racing season, it was decided that geldings could no longer compete in the Belmont Stakes or the Jockey Club Gold Cup. After Exterminator was retired, geldings were no longer eligible to run in the Saratoga Cup either.[63] While the criteria varied for the latter in subsequent years, it would be 1956 before geldings were consistently permitted to run in the race.

McDaniel quit after the horse's four-year-old campaign, and J. Simon Healey took over training duties for Exterminator's first thirteen starts in 1920. He broke track records at Jamaica in the mile-and-one-eighth Long Beach Handicap and at Aqueduct for a mile-and-a-sixteenth and set new American records in the Saratoga Cup (2:56.80) and the two-mile Autumn Gold Cup at Belmont Park (3:21.80). The latter was his fourth consecutive victory in four weeks.[64] His streak was interrupted by a loss to Sir Barton in the Saratoga Handicap in August, in which the Triple Crown winner, carrying 129 pounds, gave him 3 pounds. After the Gold Cup, McDaniel's brother Will replaced Healey.

Exterminator next won the Toronto Autumn Cup under 132 pounds before a crowd of fifteen thousand[65] and the Ontario Jockey Club Cup under 134 pounds over two and a quarter miles. He finished the season with a win in his second Pimlico Cup with a time of 3:53, breaking the track record by 20 seconds. He defeated Boniface by a neck, with Kentucky Derby winner Paul Jones back in third. In total, Exterminator won ten of seventeen races that year. He received unofficial Champion Handicap male honors.

While Exterminator was demolishing track record after track record, Americans were captivated by another chestnut horse by the name of Man o' War. Known as "Big Red," the colt had won the Preakness and Belmont Stakes and set world and track records in the Lawrence Realization and Jockey Club Gold Cup. Although Kilmer challenged owner Samuel Riddle to a $50,000 match race, Man o' War was retired after defeating Sir Barton in a match race. Exterminator had been invited to run as well, but Kilmer was reluctant to concede weight to the three-year-old under the weight-for-age conditions. Sir Barton had previously defeated Exterminator in the Saratoga Handicap.

Although he did not participate in the handicap division, Man o' War also established himself as a top weight carrier. As a two-year-old, he was assigned 130 pounds in six races, and at three, he won under as much as 138 pounds, which he carried to victory in the Potomac Handicap.

In 1921, at age six, Exterminator earned the nickname "Old Bones" from turf writer Bill Vreeland. For the season, he won eight of sixteen starts over ten different tracks, with earnings of $56,827, second only to Grey Lag. He was crowned Champion Handicapper. Still with Will McDaniel for his first five starts, he won the Long Beach Handicap in track record time but lost the Brooklyn, finishing behind Grey Lag and John P. Grier.

F. Curtis trained Exterminator to a win in the Independence Handicap at Latonia. After two third-place finishes under 135 and 132 pounds, Exterminator was reunited with his former jockey, William Knapp, this time as trainer. Exterminator won four in a row for Knapp: the Merchants' and Citizens' Handicap, the Saratoga Cup in a walkover, his second Autumn Gold Cup by six lengths under 130 pounds and his second Toronto Autumn Cup under 137 pounds. In his third Pimlico Cup, he dueled with Boniface, to whom he conceded 5 pounds, to win by a head in a "hair raising battle and finish"[66] on a muddy track. The *New York Times* provided a colorful write-up of the event:

> *A mighty roar went up from the crowd from the crowded stands as both boys sat down for the fight through the stretch. But Exterminator had enough to stand off his rival, and they flashed over the line together with the ancient warrior's head in front. The victory was a popular one, for Exterminator*

was not only the favorite in the betting but holds a warm place in the hearts of lovers of a game thoroughbred.[67]

Exterminator was named Co-Champion Older Male with Mad Hatter for 1921. In his sixth racing season, he was matched with his seventh trainer, Eugene Wayland. He won ten of seventeen starts, carried over 130 pounds in fourteen of them and led the older-horse division with earnings of $71,075. He opened the season with a victory over the sprinter Billy Kelly in the six-furlong Harford Handicap. Following a narrow loss to his old rival Boniface, he won six straight races in as many weeks: the Pimlico Spring Handicap (133), the Clark Handicap (133),[68] the Kentucky Handicap (138), the Bayside Handicap (133), the Garden City Handicap (135) and the Brooklyn Handicap (135), just three days later.

The Brooklyn was perhaps one of the gelding's greatest victories. In a thrilling stretch-drive, Exterminator ran stride for stride with Grey Lag, to whom he conceded nine pounds, to win by a head at the wire. In front of a crowd of twenty-two thousand, he ran the mile-and-one-eighth race in 1:50 and returned to "one of the most remarkable receptions ever accorded a horse on an American racecourse."[69]

Exterminator came out of the race fatigued and didn't touch his feed. He won only four of his remaining nine starts that year, but these included his fourth Saratoga Cup and third Toronto Autumn Cup. In the former, he fought off Mad Hatter (winner of the 1921 and 1922 Metropolitan and Jockey Club Gold Cup) in a stretch duel to win by half a length. He faced his heaviest impost in the Independence, where he carried 140 pounds and could manage only a sixth-place finish. At the end of the season, he received unofficial Horse of the Year honors and was voted Co-Champion Handicapper with Grey Lag.

In 1923, Exterminator only raced three times, all in the month of April, and Will Shields trained the gelding for them all. He won one, the Philadelphia Handicap, under 129 pounds. In 1924, Henry McDaniel returned and saw him win one of two races in Tijuana, Mexico, and an allowance race at Havre de Grace. Under the guidance of John I. Smith, Exterminator started four more times, winning one at Blue Bonnets. His final race came in the Queens Hotel Handicap at Canadian racetrack Dorval Park—he finished third and pulled up lame.

In total, Exterminator won half of his one hundred starts, thirty-three of them stakes races (thirty-four if the 1921 Saratoga Cup, which he won as a walkover, is counted), and was unplaced in sixteen. His total career earnings

Exterminator. *Courtesy of the National Museum of Racing and Hall of Fame.*

were $252,996, second to Zev's $313,639. He carried 130 pounds or more thirty-five times and won twenty of those times.

Retired first to Remlik Hall, then to the Court Manor Stud and, finally, to Kilmer's Sun Briar Court,[70] the chestnut grew bored, and so a Shetland pony named Peanuts was bought to keep him company. Exterminator died on

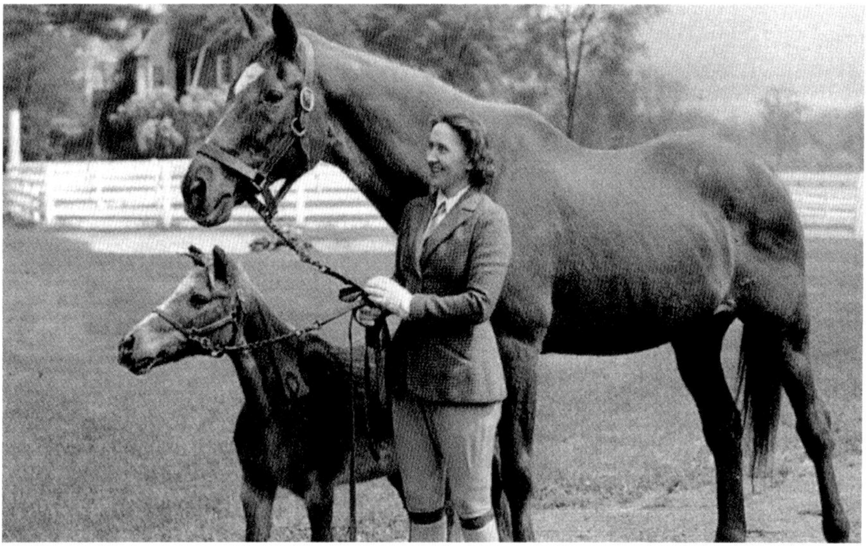

Exterminator with companion pony Peanuts. *Courtesy of the author.*

September 26, 1945,[71] at age thirty after suffering a heart attack. According to Matt Winn, he was "the greatest all-round Thoroughbred in American racing history."[72] A children's book, *Old Bones, the Wonder Horse,* was written about him and published by McGraw-Hill in 1955.

Chapter 5

Equipoise: King of the Handicap Horses

To the mind of the writer, the word gallant has always best typified Equipoise. While not built along heroic lines, he possessed a courage and a gameness that knew no limit. He was as great in defeat as in victory. He never dodged an issue, he asked no quarter, and though handicapped throughout most of his racing career with a foot that would have forced most horses to seek sanctuary long before, he bravely met all comers, carried welter weights, and was never beaten until the wire was reached.[73]

In a six-year racing career, Equipoise earned his reputation as "king of the handicap horses." He won consecutive runnings of the Metropolitan Handicap and captured the Suburban under 132 pounds. He was retrospectively named Horse of the Year for 1932 and 1933 and Champion Handicap Horse for 1932, 1933 and 1934. All this success came despite the fact that the chestnut horse suffered from chronic hoof problems. He was known to suffer from "shelly" feet and was plagued by a quarter crack throughout much of his racing career. He raced during the Depression, when purse money plummeted and racing was hit by economic hardship. His fans knew him affectionately as both "Ekky" and the "Chocolate Soldier"; as owner C.V. Whitney recalled, "Everybody loved him. His public gave him that name."[74]

Equipoise was a dark chestnut colt bred by Harry Payne Whitney. He was born at Whitney's stud farm in Lexington in 1928. He was raced for most of his career by Harry's son, Cornelius Vanderbilt (C.V.) Whitney, or "Sonny," as he was known. He was sired by Belmont Futurity winner Pennant, a son of Belmont Stakes winner and Hall of Famer Peter Pan, and out of the mare Swinging, who was by leading sire Broomstick, a son of Kentucky Derby winner Ben Brush. As a yearling, the horse did not impress Whitney Sr., who sent him to his "second-string" trainer, Fred Hopkins. Equipoise went on to exceed expectations. C.V. Whitney dedicated a whole chapter in his autobiography, *High Peaks*, to the "Chocolate Soldier."

As a child of both the Whitney and Vanderbilt families, members of America's social elite, C.V. was born into considerable wealth. His mother, Gertrude, was a daughter of Cornelius Vanderbilt, head of the New York Central Railroad lines, inherited from his grandfather and namesake. His father was the son of William C. Whitney, U.S. Secretary of the Navy and an avid polo player and racing enthusiast.

Educated at Yale, young Whitney first went to work at a Nevada mine owned by his father before becoming director of the Guaranty Trust Company of New York in 1926. A year later, he was involved in the founding of Aviation Corporation of America, which later became Pan American World Airways. He was also founder of the Hudson Bay Mining and Smelting Company Limited in Canada and was involved in the movie industry, producing the classic *Gone with the Wind*. But Sonny's true passion was horse racing, to which he was introduced in 1927, when he attended his first horse race, the Kentucky Derby, won by his father's horse Whiskery, sired by Whisk Broom II. He would go on to found the National Museum of Racing and Hall of Fame in 1950 and also served as its first president.

In total, Equipoise ran fifty-one times and won twenty-nine of them. Possessing a competitive spirit, the horse was disqualified on three occasions for bumping or biting other horses. After winning his first two starts in allowance company and then finishing third in the Aberdeen, he was unable to hit the board in the Pimlico Futurity, stumbling at the start of the race and unseating new rider Sonny Workman.[75] Equipoise went on to the New York tracks, where he proved to be nearly unbeatable and captured four straight wins,[76] including the Keene Memorial Stakes at Belmont Park, giving C.V. Whitney his first stakes win as an owner. In the Great American Stakes, he carried 130 pounds and led wire to wire.[77]

Equipoise next encountered three colts with whom he would begin great rivalries: Jamestown, Mate and Twenty Grand. Unable to catch Jamestown in the Saratoga Special, he returned to Belmont, where he suffered two more defeats—one to Mate in the Champagne, in which he was burdened with 132 pounds, and another to Jamestown in the Futurity, in which both carried 130 pounds—before winning the Eastern Shore Handicap at Havre de Grace by five lengths.[78] He saw only the heels of Twenty Grand in the Junior Champion Stakes at Aqueduct and the Kentucky Jockey Club, but in the latter, the two swept under the wire in a record time of 1:36, and Equipoise passed his rival a stride later.[79]

The chestnut colt's major triumph as a juvenile came in November in the Pimlico Futurity, in which he almost didn't start. C.V. Whitney's father had just died the week before, and it was only upon the encouragement of Whitney Sr.'s friend William Woodward that he entered the horse in the race.[80] As Whitney recalled:

> *He* [Woodward] *phoned me and urged me to go ahead. He said my father would approve. "Please run him," he said. So run him I did. Ordinarily, it would have been a happy occasion. This was the first horse to run in my name. So I traveled to Baltimore dressed in a mourning suit with a bowler hat, and with mixed emotions. But before long Equipoise had me jumping to my feet and shouting. Left behind at the post by twenty lengths, he slowly wore his field down and then won by one-half length.*[81]

Equipoise put in a spectacular performance, overcoming being left at the gate and losing two shoes to defeat Twenty Grand and Mate by half a length. Jockey Sonny Workman commented that it "may have been the greatest race anybody ever saw."[82] At year's end, Equipoise was voted the unofficial Co-Champion Two-Year-Old along with Jamestown. He ran sixteen times that season, winning nine, and was out of the money only once.

Equipoise started as the favorite for the 1931 Kentucky Derby, but after running last in the Chesapeake Stakes, it was discovered that he had a kidney aliment known as azoturio, or "blackwater." He returned to finish fourth behind Mate in the Preakness, which was run before the Derby at that time, but pulled up lame and then was retired for the rest of his three-year-old season.

As a four-year-old, Equipoise won ten of fourteen races. He began the season with wins in an overnight handicap at Bowie, the Harford at Havre de Grace and the Toboggan at Belmont. On May 21, 1932, he won the Metropolitan Handicap, defeating Sun Meadow and his old rival, Mate, returning to "thunderous applause." A 3–5 favorite, the stallion won by two and a half lengths. Ten days later, he returned to the winner's circle after racing to victory under 128 pounds in the Delavan Purse at Arlington Park, defeating 1930's champion, Jamestown, and setting a new world record for

C.V. Whitney accepts the cup from George Bull for Equipoise's victory in the Whitney Stakes on August 13, 1932, at Saratoga. *Courtesy of Keeneland-Cook.*

the mile at 1:34⅖—a record that would not be beaten for seventeen years.[83] Four days later, Equipoise won the Stars and Stripes Handicap at the same track, leading wire to wire.

After two losses at Arlington Park in July, Equipoise returned to the races at Saratoga in August, taking the Wilson Stakes by two lengths, and then led wire to wire in the Whitney, taking the win by three lengths from three-year-old Gusto to claim the trophy for the family for which it was named. According to the *New York Times*, this secured his standing as the best horse in the handicap division.

Equipoise's other significant victory that year came in the Havre de Grace Cup Handicap, in which he gave twenty-one pounds to Gallant Sir and won by a length. He closed out the season with a third-place finish in the Laurel Handicap and placed in the Washington Handicap, unable to catch the mare Tred Avon. His earnings totaled $107,375 for the season,[84] and he was voted unofficial Champion Handicap Horse and Horse of the Year.

At five, Equipoise was placed under the guidance of trainer Thomas J. Healey, for whom he won seven straight races. He took the Metropolitan for

Equipoise. *Courtesy of the National Museum of Racing and Hall of Fame.*

a second time, giving 26 pounds to the runner-up, Okaki. Four days later, he won the Suburban under 132 pounds over a mile and a quarter, defeating Osculator and Apprentice. Later that summer, he won the Hawthorne Gold Cup by two lengths, defeating Gallant Sir despite being intentionally bumped—an attempt by Al Capone to fix the race.[85] Years later, Capone personally apologized to Whitney for the incident, admitting that he had instructed his jockey to bump his horse against Equipoise because he had placed a large bet on Gallant Sir.[86]

Also in 1933, Equipoise won the Wilson Stakes for a second time; the Arlington Handicap, in which he shouldered 135 pounds, his heaviest import; the Philadelphia Handicap, which he won "going away"[87]; and the Saratoga Cup. In the latter, he raced beyond a mile and a quarter for the first time and defeated Gusto and Keep Out. At year's end, he was once again crowned Horse of the Year as well as Champion Handicapper.

In his six-year-old campaign, Equipoise won the Philadelphia Handicap for the second time at Havre de Grace, the Dixie Handicap at Pimlico and his third consecutive Metropolitan. In the latter, he carried top weight of 132 pounds and was disqualified for swerving in front of the second-place winner, Mr. Khayyam.[88] After being burdened with 134 pounds and finishing second to Ladysman in the Suburban, he was rested until the fall. In November, he defeated Faireno in the Whitney Gold Trophy, carrying 128 pounds on a wet and muddy track. At the conclusion of the racing season, he was again crowned Champion Handicapper.

At seven, Equipoise managed a second and a first in California (though he was disqualified from his win in an overnighter) before his career ended with disappointment in the Santa Anita Handicap, in which he was burdened with 130 pounds and finished seventh behind steeplechaser Azucar.

Equipoise. *Courtesy of the author.*

Equipoise was retired to stud having won twenty-nine of fifty-one starts, twenty-five of them stakes races and with career earnings of $338,610—the second-highest total to date at the time. His retirement made front-page headlines in the *Lexington-Herald* for two days straight, and a reception was held at the Whitney Farm for his fans.[89] He was ranked number twenty-one on *Blood-Horse*'s list of the top one hundred racehorses of the twentieth century. In an interview about Equipoise in 1984, C.V. Whitney wistfully commented, "People don't remember the stars of those days. Oú sont les neiges d'antan? [Where are the snows of yesteryear?]"[90]

Four years after his death, due to enteritis in 1938 at age ten, Equipoise was leading sire, partly on account of his son Shut Out, who captured the Kentucky Derby and Belmont Stakes. He produced 12 percent stakes winners in only four seasons at stud. His son Equestrian sired the great Stymie. Equipoise was inducted into the Hall of Fame in 1957. The Equipoise Mile, originally named in his honor, is a Grade III race run at Arlington Park and open to horses three years of age and up, with weight assigned. Inaugurated in 1941, it was renamed the Hanshin Cup Handicap in 2000.[91]

Chapter 6

DISCOVERY: THE IRON HORSE

Discovery is the standard by which weight carriers are judged.[92]

Discovery dominated the handicap scene in the mid-1930s. He acquired his nickname, the "Iron Horse," on account of his weight-carrying abilities. Discovery was also referred to by racegoers as the "Big Train," perhaps on account of either his stamina or in reference to the railroad industry that was both his mode of transportation and responsible for this owner's wealth. At four, Discovery won the Merchants' and Citizens' Handicap under a crippling 139 pounds and was retrospectively named Horse of the Year over Triple Crown winner Omaha. As a five-year-old, he became the first horse to be voted official American Champion Handicap Horse. He was triumphant in the Brooklyn and Whitney Handicaps on three occasions. Discovery was inducted into the Hall of Fame in 1969. In its ranking of the top one hundred racehorses of the twentieth century, Blood-Horse Publications placed him at number thirty-seven.

Discovery was born at Mereworth Farm in Lexington, Kentucky, in 1931 and bred by Walter J. Salmon Jr. He was sired by Preakness winner Display and out of the Light Brigade mare Ariadne. Unlike his sire, who was known for his temper, Discovery was a well-mannered and good-looking colt. John Hervey described him as having "a gleaming golden coat which, when the sun strikes it, gives back a glow of molten iridescence…its rich undertones are full of warmth and splendor, making it a feast for the eye as a matter of color alone."[93]

The chestnut colt was initially owned by Adolphe Pons of Maryland's Country Life Farm and trained by John R. Pryce for his juvenile season, during which he won only twice and placed in five stakes races out of fourteen starts. He was defeated on several occasions by eventual Kentucky Derby winner and Hall of Famer Cavalcade.

The colt's first start was at Belmont Park on June 3, 1933, in which he ran fourth. Five days later, he again finished fourth, this time just a nose out of the place money. After a poor performance in a maiden special weight at Arlington Park, he got his first win, victorious by five lengths on July 6, 1933, in his fourth start against other maidens.[94] After hitting the board in a couple allowance races and finishing seventh in the Arlington Futurity, he was third in the Hopeful Stakes behind Bazaar and High Quest. Discovery next won an allowance race at Havre de Grace and then was unplaced in the Eastern Shore Handicap behind High Quest and Cavalcade. Twice in a row he ran third—in the Richard Johnson Stakes at Laurel and the Breeder's Futurity at Latonia. He then managed second in the one-mile Kentucky Jockey Club Stakes.

After his thirteenth start, Discovery was bought for $25,000 by twenty-one-year-old Alfred G. Vanderbilt II, who had just acquired Sagamore Farm in Baltimore County, a birthday gift from his mother, Margaret Emerson, daughter of Bromo-Seltzer inventor Isaac E. Emerson. Trainer J.H. (Bud) Stotler advised the young multimillionaire to purchase the horse.[95] Discovery ran in one final race as a two-year-old for his new owner, finishing second in the Walden Handicap at Pimlico, behind Chicstraw but ahead of Cavalcade.

Named for his father, who died a hero in the sinking of the RMS *Lusitania*, Alfred was a first cousin of C.V. Whitney. Young Vanderbilt was an avid equestrian and had recently dropped out of Yale to turn his attention to breeding and racing Thoroughbreds full-time. Discovery would help to instill a deep passion for the sport in Vanderbilt, who remarked, "That kind of feeling you get when Discovery is at the post and everyone thinks it's all over but the shouting and you know it isn't. That's what I like about racing."[96]

After retiring for the winter in Maryland, Discovery returned at three under the guidance of a new exercise rider, Jimmy Starkey, and jockey John Bejshak. He ran third in the Chesapeake Stakes behind Cavalcade, who broke a track record. Discovery was hot on his heels in the Derby and finished second by two and a half lengths. He then ran third behind High Quest and Cavalcade in the Preakness but did not run in the Belmont. He next won an allowance race by ten lengths and then once again lost to the

Left to right: W.C. Winfrey, Eric Guerin and Alfred G. Vanderbilt II at Saratoga on August 23, 1952, after Native Dancer won the Grand Union Hotel Stakes. *Courtesy of Keeneland-Cook.*

Derby winner in the American Derby, where he finished second, and in the Detroit Derby, where he was unplaced.

Following five loses to Cavalcade, the horse's connections opted to race the colt against older horses. After a victory in a prep race, Discovery was entered in the Brooklyn Handicap. Having not yet won a stakes race, he was assigned 113 pounds, and he scampered home to a six-length win over the previous year's winner, five-year-old Dark Secret, who carried 126 pounds, and the three-year-old Acorn Stakes winner Fleam, who carried 108 pounds.

The win seemed to boost the colt's confidence, and although he suffered defeat in the Arlington Classic at the hands of his old rival Cavalcade, he went on to take the Kenner and Whitney Stakes races—the latter a weight-for-age event. These would be the first of three Brooklyn and Whitney victories for the colt. In September, he also set a world record of 1:55[97] for the one-mile-and-three-sixteenths Rhode Island Handicap under 119 pounds at Narragansett Park before a crowd of forty thousand.[98]

Discovery next won the Potomac Handicap by four lengths carrying 128 pounds. He finished third in the Havre de Grace Handicap under 126 pounds but retaliated to win the Maryland Handicap under the top weight of 130. By the end of the season, Discovery had won eight races in sixteen starts and had replaced Cavalcade in the spotlight.[99]

At four, Discovery became renowned for his ability to carry—and win—under heavy weight assignments. He won eleven of nineteen races in the 1935 season, eight of them consecutively, and was retrospectively named Champion Handicapper and Horse of the Year, beating out Omaha for the latter award—the only time a Triple Crown winner has not received the honor. That year, at twenty-three years of age, Vanderbilt became the youngest member to be elected to The Jockey Club.

His season began with a string of disappointing losses in big races: the Toboggan (fifth), Metropolitan (fourth), Suburban (second), Queen's County Handicap and Rock Park Handicap (third), but he rebounded to win his second Brooklyn Handicap, carrying 123 pounds and setting a new world record of 1:48⅕ for a mile and one eighth. He defeated Metropolitan winner King Saxon by eight lengths, as well as Omaha, back in third.

Next up was the Detroit Challenge Cup, in which Discovery faced only Azucar and won by thirty lengths,[100] equaling the track record of 1:58⅕ for a mile and three sixteenths under 126 pounds on a muddy track. In the Stars and Stripes Handicap, he won by six lengths (again carrying 126 pounds); in the Butler Handicap under 131 pounds, he won by an astounding fifteen lengths; and in the Arlington Handicap under 135 pounds, he won by five lengths and set a new track record of 2:01⅕ for a mile and a quarter. Discovery then won the Wilson Stakes, a weight-for-age race, for the first time.

In August in the Merchants' and Citizens' Handicap, Discovery shouldered 139 pounds and won before a crowd of twenty-five thousand.[101] Eleven days later, he carried the same weight and lost in the Narragansett Special. He returned to the winner's circle for the Whitney Stakes and the Hawthorne Gold Cup, carrying 126 pounds both times, before shipping to brand-new Suffolk Downs for the Massachusetts Handicap, where he carried 138 pounds and finished third to Top Row and Whopper. He capped off the season with a twelve-length victory in the Cincinnati Handicap under 132 pounds and a fourth-place finish in the Washington Handicap under 138 pounds. He won $102,545 that year.

In 1936, at five years of age, the "Iron Horse" won six of fourteen starts. At the beginning of the year, he went west to California via freight car, where he won the San Carlos under 130 pounds, finished fifth in the San Antonio under 138 pounds and finished seventh in the Santa Anita Handicap after heavy bumping. After a four-month rest, Discovery took the Inchcape Handicap under 135 pounds and then won his third Brooklyn Handicap under the heaviest weight assignment, 136 pounds. Unplaced in the Stars and the Stripes (138) and the Massachusetts (126), he won the Saratoga Handicap under 132.

Facing only his stablemate and one other rival in the Wilson, Discovery won "under stout restraint."[102] Assigned a backbreaking 143 pounds in the Merchants' and Citizens' Handicap, he finished fifth. The *New York Times* reported that his third win in the Whitney was "the most decisive victory to be scored in a big American stake in many years."[103] He lost his final three races: the Saratoga Cup, in which he carried 126, to Granville (116); the Narragansett Special, carrying 130, to Rosemont (121); and the Havre de Grace, in which he finished fifth under 130 pounds. In the paddock, after

Discovery. *Courtesy of Keeneland.*

saddling him for his last start, Stotler said, "The good Lord makes one like him every 50 years or so, and sometimes not even then."[104]

Discovery retired having won twenty-seven races (twenty-two of them stakes races) out of sixty-three starts and with career earnings of $256,326, second only to Zev as leading money winner in American racing. He returned to Sagamore Farm, where he stood at stud for twenty-one years. He sired twenty-five graded stakes winners but left a lasting legacy through his daughters. He is the broodmare sire of champions Native Dancer, Bold Ruler, Ruffian, Bed O' Roses and stakes winners Intentionally and Hasty Road. The Discovery Handicap, open to three-year-olds at a distance of a mile and one eighth, is run in the horse's honor each November at Aqueduct Racetrack.

Chapter 7

Devil Diver: The Record Holder

Devil Diver was named Champion Handicapper in 1943 and 1944. He won Kentucky's Phoenix Handicap as well as many of the major New York handicap races. He faced his heaviest impost when he carried 140 pounds to victory in an overnight handicap, and his record of winning three consecutive editions of the Metropolitan Handicap remains unbeaten. Devil Diver was inducted into the Hall of Fame in 1980. He was also inducted into the Aiken Thoroughbred Horse Racing Hall of Fame and is ranked number fifty-five in Blood-Horse's *Top 100 Racehorses of the 20th Century.* He was plagued throughout his racing career by sore feet due to a conformational flaw—the inside quarter of his off forefoot was flat instead of concave.[105]

Devil Diver was born on March 11, 1939, in Lexington, Kentucky, at Greentree Farm (now part of Gainesway Farm), owned by Mrs. Payne Whitney.[106] The dark bay colt was out of the Royal Minstrel mare Dabchick and sired by St. Germans, a stakes-winning grandson of Swynford and sire of Kentucky Derby winners Twenty Grand and Bold Venture. Harry Payne Whitney, Mrs. Payne's brother-in-law, imported St. Germans from England in 1925 for $125,000. Mrs. Whitney, born Helen Julia Hay, was a daughter of John Milton Hay, the U.S. ambassador to Great Britain and the country's Secretary of State. A poet and writer of children's books, Helen married William "Payne" Whitney, who established Greentree Stable in Red Bank, New Jersey, in 1914, named for the couple's estate on Long Island. In 1925, Greentree branched out into breeding at its Lexington farm. After her husband's death in 1927, Helen took over management of the properties.

John M. Gaver Sr. at Keeneland, 1971. *Courtesy of the* Thoroughbred Times/*Keeneland.*

Devil Diver was slow to mature—at least on the track. Nevertheless, he had a successful juvenile campaign. Under the watchful eye of trainer John M. Gaver Sr., he captured three stakes races: the Breeder's Futurity, the Hopeful and the Sanford. According to the Aiken Thoroughbred Horse Racing Hall of Fame, Devil Diver won four times out of twelve starts as a two-year-old, earning $65,359.

A graduate of Princeton University, Gaver worked as a teacher and wrestling coach at a prep school before being invited by a friend, trainer James G. Rowe, to work at Brookdale Farm and the racing stable owned by Harry Payne Whitney. Gaver joined Rowe in running Greentree Stable in 1930, and in 1939, Gaver became head trainer. Throughout his career, he trained four champions: Devil Diver; Capot, 1949 Horse of the Year; Stage Door Johnny, 1968 champion three-year-old colt; and Tom Fool, 1953 Horse of the Year. Gaver was inducted into the Hall of Fame in 1966.

Devil Diver's first start was in a five-furlong allowance race at Belmont Park in late May 1941 on the Suburban undercard. Ridden by the veteran jockey Eddie Arcaro and made the favorite at 2–1, he finished second behind the Man o' War colt Soldier Song.[107] The result was the same in his next two attempts, maiden special weights at Saratoga, both run at five and a half furlongs. Three times turned out to be the charm, however, and on August 8, piloted by Don Meade Sr., Devil Driver scampered home ahead of the field at the same track and over the same distance.

Next up was a victory in the six-furlong Sanford, followed by a third-place finish in the Grand Union Hotel Stakes, in which he first suffered defeat at the "hooves" of his stablemate, the Equipoise colt Shut Out.

Devil Diver breezes at Keeneland in 1942 in preparation for the Phoenix Handicap. *Courtesy of the Aiken Thoroughbred Racing Hall of Fame and Museum.*

Devil Diver retaliated to even the score, winning the Hopeful "going away."[108] After three second-place finishes (in the Futurity Trial, Futurity and Remsen Handicap), he returned to winning form in the Breeder's Futurity and closed out the season with a narrow loss to Contradiction in the Pimlico Futurity. It was around this time that Devil Diver began to have trouble with his right front hoof.

At three, Devil Diver was pointed toward the Derby, and in preparation, he raced against older horses in the six- furlong Phoenix Handicap[109] on April 9 at Keeneland. He led wire to wire on a muddy track and defeated the previous year's Triple Crown winner Whirlaway in a time of 1:13⅗[110] for the six furlongs. That turned out to be his only stakes win that year.

Although the colt was prepared for the Blue Grass Stakes at the end of the Keeneland meet, he did not run due to an "unusual accident" that occurred when, lying down asleep in his stall, he was startled by the sound of a car horn and leapt abruptly to his feet, cutting his left hind leg.[111] On Derby day, under the expert guidance of Arcaro, who chose the mount over eventual winner Shut Out, Devil Diver could manage only sixth, finishing behind his stablemate whom he had beaten on four previous occasions. Both colts floundered in the Preakness, with the Derby winner running fifth and Devil Diver back in eighth place at the wire. Devil Diver won two overnighters and an allowance race later that season, was third in the Jerome and also placed in the Vosburgh Stakes.[112]

Perhaps one of the horse's most stellar performances in 1942 came at Aqueduct on September 7 in a five-and-a-half-furlong handicap, in which he carried 140 pounds and "drew away"[113] for a decisive win over Dogpatch, yet the event received little mention in race write-ups. His preparation for both the Withers Stakes and the Kent Stakes at Delaware Park was halted due to issues with his bad heel. He concluded the season with a disappointing finish in the Continental Handicap at Jamaica in October. Gaver led the nation in earnings for the year. Devil Diver spent the winter in the South preparing for an early spring campaign.

In 1943, Devil Diver emerged as a mature horse and a force to be reckoned with on the top tracks in New York. That year, he won his first of three Metropolitan Handicaps at Belmont Park and also took the Toboggan, Carter and Brooklyn Handicaps for a total of four victories in nine starts. In the Toboggan, Devil Diver carried 116 pounds on opening day at Belmont and was given a slashing ride by jockey George Woolf to take the win over With Regards by a length.[114] The time of 1:10 for the six-furlong event was just off the stake record, held by Equipoise (carrying 129 pounds), who ran the race in 1932 over the Widener course in a time of 1:09⅗.[115] Five days later, the four-year-old horse took the one-mile Metropolitan over Marriage under 117 pounds in a time of 1:36⅗.[116]

Devil Diver came up short in the mile-and-a-quarter Suburban, finishing fifth under 121 pounds. In the Carter, Devil Diver again took the victory over Marriage, this time carrying 126 pounds over seven furlongs in a dramatic photo finish that saw him get the win by a head. The two horses were described as "coming with a tremendous rush in the last furlong…in a kind of race that will linger long in the memory of those who saw it."[117]

In the Brooklyn, the bay scored an upset victory under Steve Brooks by defeating favorite Shut Out, finishing just two seconds off the track record and a length and a half in front. Running off the pace this time, he carried 123 pounds.[118] The race was most impressive as it was the first time he had won at a distance greater than one mile. His victories in the Toboggan, Metropolitan and Brooklyn in one season constituted an unprecedented triple.[119]

The four-year-old horse was next shipped to Chicago for the mile-and-one-eighth Stars and Stripes Handicap. It was not to be, however, as the horse struggled to a fifth-place finish; after the race, it was discovered that he had injured one of his front feet. He was retired for the season.[120] At year's end, Devil Diver was voted Champion Handicap Male Horse by the *Daily Racing Form*. *Turf and Sport Digest* named Market Wise as Champion.

At five, Devil Diver had his most stellar racing season, though he ran for much of the year with a bar plate to protect his right forefoot.[121] Under the guidance of Ted Atkinson, he was triumphant for the first time in two tries in the Paumanok Handicap, in which he narrowly defeated Calumet Farms' Apache. He scored repeat victories in the Toboggan and Metropolitan, carrying 134 pounds in both, a weight record for the winner in the latter, in which he ran the mile in 1:35⅘ to defeat Alquest and Boysey.[122] He was scratched from the Suburban on the morning of the race when his troublesome heel became sore and pus was found to have formed in it.[123] The bay horse returned in July to win the American Legion Handicap followed by the Whitney Stakes, in which he defeated Princequillo by half a length.[124] Burdened with 135 pounds in the Saratoga Handicap, Devil Diver could not hit the board. Under a light 117 pounds, he won the Wilson, but he lost the Narragansett Special under 130 pounds.

The 1944 Manhattan Handicap was an odd event, as relayed by writer Joe Palmer. It began with a false start when the gate in front of one of the starters, Caribou, did not open. Devil Diver pushed his gate open with his nose and broke slowly. Another horse's gate opened only partway. A replacement gate was then sent for, and in a second try, all horses broke cleanly. With many of the jockeys having been instructed to avoid early speed, the fractions for the first two quarters were very slow—in fact, a trotting horse, Greyhound, had previously run the time for the second quarter of 28 ⅘![125] It was only in the last half mile of the race that the horses started moving, and Devil Diver pulled away to win by more than a length with a time of 2:36⅗, astonishingly just nine seconds off Bolingbroke's track record for the distance.

In the midst of celebration, misfortune occurred. The day after his victory in the Manhattan, Devil Diver's owner, Mrs. Payne Whitney, died. Greentree Stable continued on under the direction of her son and daughter, Joan and Jock Whitney, with Devil Diver carrying its pink-and-black silks to the post. Only a week after his victory in the Manhattan, the Diver ran third in the Jockey Club Gold Cup. He ran unplaced in the Gallant Fox Handicap at Jamaica a few weeks later, and he lost the Pimlico Special in November to Calumet Farm's filly Twilight Tear.

In the Special, Devil Diver carried 126 pounds to Twilight Tear's 117 and could not catch the first female horse to ever compete in the race. The filly went right to the lead from the gate and won by six lengths in a time of 1:56⅗, matching Seabiscuit's stakes record and only one-fifth off the track record for a mile and three-sixteenths.[126]

At the end of the season, Devil Diver had won seven races, carrying more than 130 pounds in every race, and was once again crowned Champion Handicapper. The initial plan was to retire the horse at the end of the season (and in fact, his stud book was already filled), but in the absence of other stakes and handicap starters, Greentree made the decision to return him to the races in 1945. Instead of heading to the breeding shed, Devil Diver was shipped off to Greentree's winter training base in Aiken, South Carolina.

The bay horse returned for a fifth year of racing at age six. He started off with a second win in the Paumanok Handicap, carrying 132 pounds. He was second to Apache (129) in the Toboggan, lugging 135 pounds on a sloppy track, but returned five days later to win his third Metropolitan,

Devil Diver winning the Paumanok Handicap at Jamaica Racecourse on May 24, 1945. *Courtesy of the* Thoroughbred Times/*Keeneland*.

this time carrying 129 pounds. A week later, he finally won the mile-and-a-quarter Suburban, the middle jewel of New York's Handicap Triple Crown, carrying top weight of 132 pounds and giving 13 pounds to the champion Stymie. Ridden by Eddie Arcaro, the bay led all the way and finished in a time of 2:04.[127] His last start came in the Brooklyn, where he carried 132 pounds and was defeated by Stymie, to whom he conceded 16 pounds.

Devil Diver joins Grey Lag, Buckpasser and Forego as the only horses to win all three races of the New York Handicap Triple in different years. He is also one of only three horses (the others being Equipoise and Eight Thirty) to have won another "triple," this one consisting of the Toboggan, Metropolitan and Suburban, albeit in different years.[128] To date, no horse has won all three races in the same season.

In August, Devil Diver was retired after reinjuring his right front hoof in a workout at Belmont. He retired with twenty-two wins in forty-seven starts and with earnings of $261,064. At stud at Greentree Farm, he sired eighteen

Devil Diver with Eddie Arcaro up. *Courtesy of the* Thoroughbred Times/*Keeneland.*

stakes winners, including Anchors Aweigh, Fleet Diver (dam of Champion Handicapper Native Diver), Call Over and Beau Diable. He died in 1961 after fracturing a leg.

Chapter 8

Tom Fool: Horse of the Decade

Tom Fool's story is that of a colt who was highly regarded from the time he was foaled and, remarkably enough, turned out to be fully as capable as he looked.[129]

Tom Fool was the second of only four horses to lay claim to the New York Handicap Triple Crown: the Metropolitan, Suburban and Brooklyn. He won at distances ranging from five and a half furlongs to a mile and a quarter and under imposts as heavy as 136 pounds. He won three championships in 1953: Horse of the Year, Champion Older Horse and Champion Sprinter. He is ranked number eleven in *Thoroughbred Champions: Top 100 Racehorses of the 20th Century*.

Tom Fool was born on March 31, 1949, at Manchester Farm, near Lexington. He was bred by Duval Headley and owned by the Whitney family's Greentree Stables, which purchased him privately as a yearling for $20,000. Trainer John M. Gaver Sr. had gone to inspect the colt on behalf of John Hay Whitney, co-owner of Greentree, with his sister, Mrs. (Joan Whitney) Charles S. Payson, and was impressed despite the fact that he was slightly toed out. Whitney approved the sale even after Tom Fool cut his leg on the paddock fence only a few days after Gaver had gone to see him.

The dark bay horse was sired by the 1937 juvenile champion Menow, whom Headley had trained. Menow had defeated War Admiral in the 1938 Massachusetts Handicap and sired Horse of the Year Capot, who also raced for Greentree. Tom Fool was the second foal out of the Bull Dog mare Gaga, who was out of a mare by Equipoise. Headley had purchased the unraced Gaga for a mere $2,250; she won several allowance sprints for him.

The year Tom Fool was born, his half sister Aunt Jinny (Heliopolis) was named Champion Two-Year-Old filly. His third dam, Laughing Queen, was sired by two-time Eclipse Champion Sun Briar. Tom Fool stood 15.3 hands and was described as having a lovely disposition. The horse had an unusual way of going, as was relayed in the 1954 *American Racing Manual*: "When he is in action, he thrusts both forelegs forward and both hind legs behind him for all the world like a horse clearing a hedge."[130]

Artist Richard Stone Reeves, who was commissioned to paint many of racing's equine greats, had the following to say about Tom Fool: "[He] was an archetype of the American handicap horse...He was docile and well-mannered with a finely chiseled head and large kind eyes that reflected his disposition. Tom Fool instinctively caught the attention of several veteran horsemen, who admired his conformation, particularly his broad chest and strong, straight legs."[131]

Canadian jockey Ted Atkinson rode Tom Fool in all thirty of his career starts. Atkinson was born in Toronto in 1916 but moved to the United States with his family when he was three. He started riding at age twenty-one and led all jockeys with 287 wins in 1944. In 1946, he led the list again and became the first jockey whose mounts earned more than $1 million in one year.

Well liked by his fellow riders and other horsemen, Atkinson had a number of nicknames, including "the Gentleman," "the Professor" (he was known to have a love of classical literature) and "the Slasher," for his style of whipping his horses directly on their rump in an up-and-down action. Atkinson disliked the latter nickname and claimed that he never left marks on his horses or abused them in any way. The story goes that a trainer he rode for preferred this method and did not want his horses touched on the flanks. Horses whipped on the rump are less likely to swerve on the track and interfere with the action of other runners.[132]

In 1947, Atkinson became the contract rider for Greentree Stable. He was the recipient of the George Woolf Memorial Jockey Award in 1957, the year in which he was also inducted into the Hall of Fame. George Woolf had died in a riding accident in 1946, and Atkinson had been riding the horse next to him when his horse fell.[133] In 2002, he was inducted into the Canadian Horse Racing Hall of Fame.

At two, Tom Fool had a late start to racing due to cracked heels. He would go on to win five times in seven starts, finishing second in two. The colt won

R O S E B E N

Portrait of Roseben by artist Heather Rohde. Quote on bottom of the piece reads, "Known as 'The Big Train,' he was the greatest sprinter of his time."—S. Call. *Courtesy of the artist (www.rohdefineart.com).*

R O A M E R

Portrait of Roamer by artist Heather Rohde. Quote on the bottom of the piece reads, "He is as smart as they come but honest as the day is long. He will give up to the last ounce of speed he has on tap."—A. Shuttinger. *Courtesy of the artist (www.rohdefineart.com).*

EXTERMINATOR

Portrait of Exterminator by artist Heather Rohde. Quote on the bottom of the piece reads, "Everyone loves and reverences this brave and noble creature, and he will be remembered as long as generous hearts warm to brave and noble deeds."—G. Herring. *Courtesy of the artist (www.rohdefineart.com)*.

E Q U I P O I S E

Portrait of Equipoise by artist Heather Rohde. Quote on the bottom of the piece reads, "[The Chocolate Soldier] could run on courage alone."—T. Healey. *Courtesy of the artist (www.rohdefineart.com).*

D I S C O V E R Y

Portrait of Discovery by artist Heather Rohde. Quote on the bottom of the piece reads, "There is no other horse in turf history that ever attempted to do anything so tremendous or came anywhere near to Discovery in doing it so successfully."—J. Hervey. *Courtesy of the artist (www.rohdefineart.com)*.

DEVIL DIVER

Portrait of Devil Diver by artist Heather Rohde. Quote on the bottom of the piece reads, "Greatness is revealed not by the lights that shine upon you but by the light that shines within you."—R. Davis. *Courtesy of the artist (www.rohdefineart.com).*

TOM FOOL

Portrait of Tom Fool by artist Heather Rohde. Quote on the bottom of the piece reads, "It seemed as though he could break a record at every pole."—T. Atkinson. *Courtesy of the artist (www.rohdefineart.com)*.

KELSO

Portrait of Kelso by artist Heather Rohde. Quote on the bottom of the piece reads, "There has probably never been another horse before or since who has dominated racing for such a long period as Kelso."—C. Dulay. *Courtesy of the artist (www.rohdefineart.com).*

D A M A S C U S

Portrait of Damascus by artist Heather Rohde. Quote on the bottom of the piece reads, "He danced all the dances and ran all the distances...never did we see him spit out the bit."—C. Hatton. *Courtesy of the artist (www.rohdefineart.com).*

F O R E G O

Portrait of Forego by artist Heather Rohde. Quote on the bottom of the piece reads, "There is a quality that manifests itself in stress of competition. It is called valor. It commands the respect of all, wherever found, in friend or foe, man or horse. Forego had it."—*Blood-Horse* magazine. *Courtesy of the artist (www.rohdefineart.com).*

Forego's grave at the Kentucky Horse Park. *Courtesy of the author.*

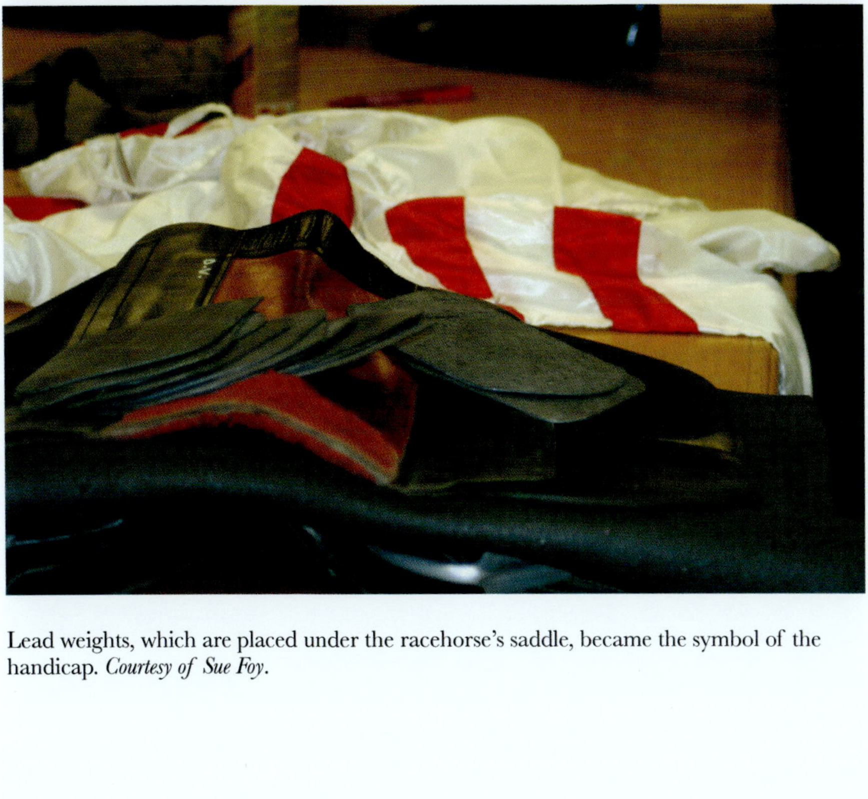

Lead weights, which are placed under the racehorse's saddle, became the symbol of the handicap. *Courtesy of Sue Foy.*

Churchill Downs, site of the Clark Handicap and Louisville Handicap. *Courtesy of the author.*

Statue at Churchill Downs commemorating 2006 Kentucky Derby winner Barbaro, descendant of Discovery. *Wikimedia Commons.*

Belmont Park, the current site of the New York Handicap Triple series of races, which is composed of the Metropolitan, Brooklyn and Suburban Handicaps. *Courtesy of Cindy Dulay/Horse-Races.net.*

Curlin, two-time winner of the Jockey Club Gold Cup and one of only two Champion Older Male horses to win carrying more than 124 pounds since 1998. *Courtesy of Cindy Dulay/Horse-Races.net.*

Santa Anita Park in Arcadia, California, site of the Santa Anita Handicap, one of the few original handicaps that remains as such today. *Wikimedia Commons*.

Forego. *Courtesy of the author.*

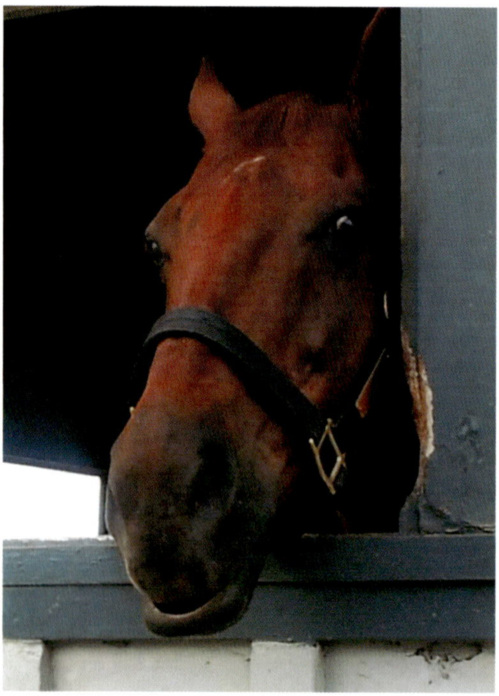

Funny Cide, 2003 Kentucky Derby winner and descendant of Tom Fool. *Courtesy of the author.*

Tom Fool with Ted Atkinson aboard. *Courtesy of the Canadian Horse Racing Hall of Fame.*

at first asking, taking a maiden race by four lengths at Saratoga on August 13, 1951. A week later, he returned to the winner's circle after capturing the Sanford Stakes at odds of 4–5, winning by a little over two lengths from First Refusal.[134] In the Grand Union Stakes, he beat Cousin by a length, but the results were reversed in the Hopeful, with Cousin defeating Tom Fool. Both carried 122 pounds. Tom Fool had two excuses for his first loss. On an off track, he wore plain plates instead of calks and seemed unable to gain traction in the footing. He had also received a tetanus shot after skinning his knee in his stall, and it is suspected that a reaction to the vaccine may have been responsible for him being off his form.[135]

In a prep race for the Futurity, he encountered traffic and finished second, four lengths behind Calumet's future Kentucky Derby winner Hill Gail. He rebounded to win the Futurity by a length and three-quarters over Primate[136] at odds of 6–1, fourth choice in the betting.[137] Next up, on a sloppy track, Tom Fool was victorious in the mile-and-one-sixteenth East View Stakes at Jamaica, defeating Put Out by a neck. He ended his juvenile season with earnings of $155,960[138] and was voted Champion Two-Year-Old Colt. He was also ranked as the highweight at 126 pounds on the Experimental Free Handicap.[139]

After wintering at Aiken, Tom Fool started his three-year-old season as an early favorite for the Kentucky Derby with a win in a six-furlong sprint at Jamaica on April 7. After running with a fever in the Wood Memorial, he finished a close second behind Master Fiddle. Tom Fool was sidelined and missed the Triple Crown races, but he returned to the track later that season and won six races in thirteen starts.

After a narrow loss to Hitex in the six-furlong overnight Rippey Handicap, followed by a fourth-place finish in a prep race for the Arlington Classic,[140] the bay colt won the Wilson Stakes under 106 pounds at a mile against older horses. A narrow loss to Count Flame in a mile-and-one-eighth overnight—the Caughnawaga Purse—was followed by a third-place finish behind Belmont Stakes winner and eventual Horse of the Year One Count and Armageddon in the Travers on a sloppy track. Tom Fool faded in the stretch after leading most of the way.

His next start came in the Jerome Handicap, but this was preceded by an incident that could have ended much worse than it did. The night before the race, the colt became cast in his stall and injured his hock in the process of righting himself. Miraculously, he recovered from the trauma to win by seven lengths over Marcador and the three-year-old Mark-Ye-Well. Next up was the one-mile Sysonby Handicap, which he won "easily" under 126 pounds,[141] defeating Alerted and Greek Ship.

Relocating to Jamaica, Tom Fool was defeated by Quiet Step in the Roamer Handicap, in which he carried 126 pounds and conceded 13 to the winner. He retaliated to take the mile-and-one-eighth Grey Lag Handicap by a nose over Battlefield a week later, carrying 119 pounds. The nine furlongs was run in 1:49⅖, just a fifth of a second shy of the track record set the year before by the four-year-old Bryan G.[142] Battlefield got the better of him the next time the two met, racing the same distance in the Westchester, with Tom Fool carrying 125 pounds to Battlefield's 123. In his final start of the season, Tom Fool won the Empire City Handicap under 128 pounds. He finished out of the money only once, running fourth in an allowance race at Arlington Park, and his earnings for the season totaled $157,850.[143]

At four, Tom Fool was undefeated in ten starts. In the words of a *Blood-Horse* staff member, "Prelude was really what Tom Fool's career was prior to 1953. In that year he was four-mature, knowing, willing, a courageous competitor blessed with commanding physical strength and trained with precision."[144]

He carried 130 pounds in both the Joe Palmer and Metropolitan Handicaps; 128 pounds in the Suburban; 135 pounds in the Carter, in which he equaled Aqueduct's seven-furlong track record of 1:22; and 136 pounds in the mile-and-a-quarter Brooklyn. He also beat Capot's track record in the mile-and-three-sixteenths Pimlico Special, which he won by eight lengths, turning in a time of 1:55⅘. His victory in the latter was ranked number twenty-seven in the book *Horse Racing's Top 100 Moments*.

In his first start of the season, the five-and-a-half-furlong Sation Handicap at Jamaica, Tom Fool, odds on at 95–100, won by two and a half lengths under 128 pounds, defeating Do Report, to whom he conceded 12 pounds. Next up was the Joe Palmer Handicap at Belmont, and he ran the six furlongs in 1:11⅗, winning by a length and a half. Then it was time for the Triple. In the one-mile Metropolitan, he took the lead after six furlongs on a somewhat sloppy track and kept it to the wire, winning by half a length over Royal Vale and finishing in a time of 1:35⅘.

The mile-and-a-quarter Suburban came just a week later, and again the Fool held off Royal Vale, to whom he conceded four pounds, to win by a nose in a time of 2:00⅗. The race was the only occasion Tom Fool was not odds-on. After the race, Atkinson was quoted as saying, "Not that he's ever run a bad race, but today's was his best. He was so full of run for the first seven-eighths, he could have beaten all track records. I asked him to run just before we entered the straightaway, and he responded."[145] The *New York Times* considered it the best race of his career, and Atkinson kissed the colt on the nose in the winner's circle, saying, "If he would have lost, I still would have kissed him after a performance like that! For seven furlongs it seemed as though he could break a record at every pole. That's how handy he was."[146]

In the Carter, Tom Fool closed on the leader, Squared Away, at the top of the stretch to win by two lengths as the 13–20 favorite. In the Brooklyn, only win bets were accepted, and he coasted home to win by one and a half lengths over Golden Gloves in 2:04⅖, the first horse since Whisk Broom II, forty years before, to win the handicap trilogy. Jockey Nick Wall, aboard the second-place finisher, was quoted as saying, "You just can't beat horses like that—no matter what the weights are."[147]

Tom Fool's last four starts came in weight-for-age races, all betless exhibitions, and he carried 126 pounds in all. He won the one-mile Wilson Stakes at Saratoga by eight lengths over Indian Land (117), his only competition; the mile-and-a-quarter Whitney over Combat Boots (114) by three and a half; his second Sysonby by three; and the Pimlico Special by eight.

Tom Fool wins the 1953 Whitney. *Courtesy of the author.*

The Sysonby that year was run in late September instead of the first week of October, its purse increased from $20,000 to $50,000, and conditions changed to a weight-for-age event, all in the hopes of a meeting between Tom Fool and Native Dancer.[148] There had been media hype about such an event throughout the summer, and there was much debate over which was the better horse. A grandson of Discovery, Native Dancer raced for Alfred G. Vanderbilt's Sagamore Farm. At two, the "Grey Ghost," as he became known, was undefeated and crowned Horse of the Year, and his only loss at three had come in the Kentucky Derby. Because of the weight allowances, Tom Fool would carry 126 pounds and Native Dancer 119.

Native Dancer came out of a victory in the American Derby with a sore left front foot that delayed his training for the big race. In early September, he returned to the track, but after a few gallops, he remained sore, indicating that he had not healed from the removal of stone bruises from the bottom of his foot. On September 12, Vanderbilt announced that he would not run; a week later, it was decided to retire him for the season. The two colts never did meet, and Greentree sent Tom Fool out to chase down Alerted and the three-year-old filly Grecian Queen—both of whom he defeated, winning by three lengths.

Although he was set to start in the mile-and-five-furlong Empire Gold Cup, Whitney announced Tom Fool's retirement shortly after the Pimlico Special.[149] Racing secretary John B. Campbell assigned him a whopping 148 pounds in the Fall Highweight; with Atkinson layed up after a fall, he did not start. At year's end, Tom Fool secured Horse of the Year honors over Champion Three-Year-Old Native Dancer, who won nine out of ten starts and earned twice as much money.

Tom Fool retired with twenty-one wins (eighteen of them stakes races), seven seconds and one third in thirty starts. His career earnings totaled $570,165.[150] He was inducted into the Hall of Fame in 1960. That same year, the National Turf Writers Association elected him Horse of the Decade. He beat out champions Nashua, Swaps and Native Dancer for the honor.[151]

The bay stallion was syndicated for $1.75 million in 1958, with Greentree retaining fifteen of thirty-five shares.[152] Though a reluctant breeder, he went on to sire thirty-four stakes winners (13 percent), including Horse of the Year and Hall of Fame inductee Buckpasser and Kentucky Derby and Preakness winner Tim Tam. Tom Fool is also the broodmare sire of Kentucky Derby winner Foolish Pleasure. He was leading sire of two-year-olds in the United States,[153] as well as leading broodmare sire in Great Britain and Ireland in 1965. The following year, he was third on the general sires list. He died on August 20, 1976, at Greentree Stud.

The Tom Fool Handicap, formerly hosted at Belmont Park, is run annually in March at Aqueduct Racetrack. It is a six-furlong race for horses three years of age and older, and weight is assigned.

Tom Fool. *Wikipedia.*

When asked to identify the best horse he ever rode, Ted Atkinson responded, "Tom Fool. His record shows it. He set records with higher handicaps. In the 19 years that I have been riding, few horses have been asked to carry the weights that Tom Fool carried as a 4-year-old. When you talk about the great horses of all time, never forget Tom Fool."[154]

Chapter 9

KELSO: KING KELLY

Once upon a time there was a horse named Kelso—but only once.[155]

Winner of ten Eclipse Awards—including an unprecedented five Horse of the Year titles—an accomplishment that is ranked third in *Horse Racing's Top 100 Moments*, Kelso is ranked fourth in *Thoroughbred Champions: Top 100 Racehorses of the 20th Century.* Kelso won thirteen times carrying 130 pounds, won five consecutive runnings of the two-mile Jockey Club Gold Cup and became the third horse to win New York's Handicap Triple Crown. He was inducted into the Hall of Fame in 1967. Jockey Eddie Arcaro, who rode the horse in fourteen of his races, claimed he had "never ridden a better horse."[156] The great horse had his own fan club, known as the Kelsolanders, and received fan mail at Woodstock Farm. In the words of David Alexander, "He's done more things better on more occasions over a longer period of time than any other horse in history."[157]

Kelso was born on April 4, 1957, at Claiborne Farm in Paris, Kentucky. He was bred by Allaire du Pont and raced for her Bohemia Stable. The Du Pont family, no strangers to horse racing, are perhaps best known outside the racing scene for their chemical company that was founded as a gunpowder mill in the early nineteenth century. Mrs. Du Pont, born Helena Allaire Crozer, married Richard Chichester Du Pont, co-founder of All-American Aviation, forerunner to U.S. Airways, in 1934. During World War II, he managed the glider program for the U.S. Army Air Force. Tragically, Du

Pont died in 1943 when his glider crashed during a demonstration flight and his parachute failed.

Kelso was sired by Your Host and out of the mare Maid of Flight. Two of Your Host's grandsires, Hyperion and Mahmoud, were Epsom Derby winners. Maid of Flight was a daughter of Triple Crown winner Count Fleet and a granddaughter of Man o' War. She was voted Broodmare of the Year in 1965, partly on account of Kelso's successes. Your Host had been a successful handicapper himself before breaking his shoulder. The injury took months to heal and left the stallion with a limp and unable to fully bend his knee. As a weanling, he had injured his upper spine, resulting in a crooked neck that caused him to run with his head low and turned to one side.

As a foal, Kelso was scrawny looking and didn't attract much attention. Only a few weeks after his birth, he was sent to Mrs. Du Pont's Woodstock Farm in Maryland. He was named for Mrs. Kelso Everett, a good friend of Mrs. Du Pont, who was known for being a perfect hostess; thus the name was a play off the name of the horse's sire. In training, under the guidance of veterinarian Dr. John Lee, the bay colt became known for his nasty temperament, biting anyone who dared cross his path and bucking off riders. He was gelded because of a testicle that interfered with his movement. He retained much of his personality, but Mrs. Du Pont had a soft spot for him, feeding him sugar and ice cream.

Richard Stone Reeves offered the following description of the champion:

> *Never known for his beauty, Kelso was of medium size, no more than 16 hands at the most, and not heavily muscled. He at times looked rather fragile for so many hard campaigns over the years. He had a dark bay coat. His head was lean and long with a fine muzzle and large bright eyes. He possessed a knowing, intelligent look and was interesting to watch when he was grazed. You then realized what a great horse you were looking at.*[158]

Kelso dominated horse racing when it was still one of the most popular sports in the United States along with baseball and boxing. As a two-year-old, the gelding developed a stifle problem and suffered frequent bouts of colic. His first start came in a six-furlong maiden event on September 4, 1959, at Atlantic City Racecourse, in which he was ridden by John Black. He passed the leaders in the stretch to win by a length and a quarter. Ten days later, he returned to the same track to finish second behind Dress Up. The 9–5 favorite in his third start, he again finished second, this time behind Windy Sands.[159]

As a three-year-old, Kelso won eight of nine starts and was voted champion of his division as well as Horse of the Year (the first three-year-old who did not win a Triple Crown race to receive this honor) and became the second gelding after Armed to earn the title. He got a late start to the season, winning a six-furlong sprint allowance at Monmouth Park on June 22 by ten lengths, with Bill Hartack aboard for new trainer Carl Hanford.

A native of Fairbury, Nebraska, Hanford was born into a racing family; both he and two of his brothers became jockeys. He won the first race ever run at Suffolk Downs in 1935[160] but was not overly successful, so he switched to training in 1939. He was inducted into the Hall of Fame in 2006. Upon receiving his award, he credited the great gelding that brought him fame. "I am here because of one horse and one horse only," he said. "I had a few stakes winners before, but they didn't compare with Kelso."[161]

Kelso next scored a twelve-length victory at Aqueduct, in which he ran a mile in 1:34⅕, believed to be a record for a three-year-old at that distance.[162] In the Arlington Classic, Kelso got stuck behind horses and finished eighth behind T.V. Lark, his only loss that year. He rebounded to win six in a row and began an eleven-race winning streak that would last until the following summer. He won the Choice Stakes, with Bill Hartack aboard, and then Eddie Arcaro rode him to victories in the Jerome and Discovery Handicaps. He then won the Lawrence Realization Stakes, in which he matched the track record of 2:40.80 for a mile and five eighths;[163] the mile-and-a-quarter Hawthorne Gold Cup; and the Jockey Club Gold Cup, in which he set a North American record time of 3:19⅖ for two miles over a sloppy track.[164] The latter two were against older horses. In the Lawrence Realization, he equaled Man o' War's time of 2:40⅘ for a mile and five eighths. On Kelso's performance in the Jockey Club Gold Cup, Arcaro remarked, "There's no doubt about it. He's the best horse in America today. He can beat anything at any distance."[165]

In 1961, Kelso became the third horse to win the New York Handicap Triple, joining Whisk Broom II and Tom Fool. In the Metropolitan, he was assigned 130 pounds and won by a neck. In the Brooklyn, he carried 136 pounds—which matches that carried by Discovery and Tom Fool and remains the highest impost assigned a winner of the race—and still managed to defeat Divine Comedy, to whom he conceded 23 pounds. He carried 133 pounds in the Suburban and won by five lengths over Nickel Boy.[166] Kelso also won the Whitney (he ran second, but the winner, Our Hope, was disqualified); the Woodward, in which he defeated that year's Kentucky Derby winner, Carry Back, and matched the track record for ten

Kelso. *Courtesy of the author.*

furlongs set by Whisk Broom II in the 1913 Suburban;[167] and his second Jockey Club Gold Cup.

In his first try on turf, Kelso finished second behind T.V. Lark in the D.C. International. At year's end, he had won seven of nine starts, was voted Champion Older Horse and earned Horse of the Year honors for the

Kelso. *Courtesy of the author.*

second time—the first horse since Whirlaway to earn consecutive titles. He would receive both awards three more times (1962–64), the first horse to win it more than twice.

Kelso returned in May 1962 for his five-year-old season after suffering from a virus.[168] He carried 133 pounds in the Met Mile, conceding 10 pounds to Carry Back, and finished in sixth place. He retaliated to win an allowance race and then finished second in the Suburban and Monmouth Handicaps behind Beau Purple and Carry Back. Bill Shoemaker, who replaced the retired Eddie Arcaro, rode him in all three races. The jockey's riding style didn't match with the headstrong Kelso, and so Ismael "Milo" Valenzuela was next given a try in the tack.

The pair won a turf allowance at Saratoga. After a fourth-place finish in another turf race, ridden by Don Pierce, Kelso won three straight: the Stymie Handicap; the Woodward, which he took by four and a half lengths over champion three-year-old Jaipur;[169] and his third Gold Cup, demolishing the field by ten lengths and breaking Nashua's record of two wins in the race. A second-place finish behind Beau Purple in the Man o' War Stakes was followed by similar results in the D.C. International, in which Match II passed him in the stretch after he had successfully held off Carry Back and Beau Purple. He won his last start that season, the inaugural Governor's Plate at Garden State, by five lengths in 2:30⅕ (a track record for the mile-and-a-half event), for a total of six wins in twelve starts. He surpassed the million-dollar earnings mark, a record at the time.

After a brief rest, Kelso was sent to Florida to begin his six-year-old season. In four starts in the state, he won both the Seminole and Gulfstream Park Handicaps, carrying 130 pounds in the latter. That year he also won the John B. Campbell Handicap at Bowie (131); the Nassau County (132); his second Suburban (133); his second Whitney Stakes; the Aqueduct (134); his third Woodward, in which he defeated top handicapper Never Bend; and a fourth Jockey Club Gold Cup. At the track watching her horse go to the post for the Gold Cup, Mrs. Du Pont stated, "[He] has proved he can carry weight and run in track record time. He has taken on every challenger and taken them all in stride. He is wonderfully consistent. He just goes on and on."[170]

However, three tries in the D.C. International did not prove to be a charm, as Kelso finished second yet again, this time behind Mongo. In total, he won nine of twelve starts, winning six consecutive stakes carrying 130 pounds or more,[171] and earned $569,762, his largest single-season total.[172]

As a seven-year-old, the bay gelding ran unplaced in the Los Angeles Handicap and Californian Stakes, likely unsettled from a long plane ride and the noisy loudspeaker set up outside his stall at Hollywood Park. Returning east, he won an overnight handicap under 136 pounds and then ran second in both the Suburban Handicap, conceding 15 pounds to the winner, Iron Peg, and the Monmouth Handicap, conceding 3 pounds to winner Mongo. After hitting his head on the starting gate, Kelso was defeated by new rival Gun

Bow in the Brooklyn. He made it to the wire in front for the Aqueduct only to be beaten by a nose in the Woodward by the grandson of War Admiral. He next won his fifth Gold Cup by five and a half lengths, the winner's purse making him the leading money earner in Thoroughbred horse racing.[173]

In the D.C. International, Kelso passed Gun Bow with a half mile to go to win the once-elusive race by four and a half lengths in a time of 2:23⅘ for a mile and a half—an American record. He ended the year with five wins in eleven starts.

In 1965, Kelso started six times and won three of them—the Diamond State Handicap, his third Whitney Stakes and the Stymie Handicap—before ending the season early due to an eye infection. He started once as a nine-year-old in a six-furlong overnight race at Hialeah Park in preparation for the Donn Handicap at Gulfstream, in which he finished fourth, but then fractured the inside sesamoid of his right front foot after a workout and was retired.

In an eight-year racing career, the gelding set nine track records and three American records and still holds the world record for two miles on dirt with a time of 3:19.1 in the 1964 Jockey Club Gold Cup. He retired as racing's all-time leading money earner, with career earnings of $1,977,896, surpassing the record achieved by Round Table. The record held for fourteen years until beaten by Affirmed in 1979. Kelso started sixty-three times, won thirty-nine races and finished out of the money just ten times. The *Blood-Horse* wrote a retirement tribute to the gallant gelding, stating, "Kelso demonstrated the durability of class. No horse in our time was so good, so long. His was mature greatness."[174]

Kelso went on to a second career as a hunter jumper and also enjoyed fox hunting with Mrs. Du Pont. On October 15, 1983, at twenty-seven years of age, Kelso, along with Forego and John Henry, was paraded in front of a crowd of over thirty-two thousand before the start of the Jockey Club Gold Cup at Belmont Park. It would be his last public appearance, however, as he died of colic the next day and was buried in the equine cemetery at Woodstock Farm. The epitaph on his gravestone reads, "Where he Gallops, the Earth Sings."

The Kelso Stakes is a Grade II one-mile event for horses aged three years and up, run on the dirt each fall since 1988 at Belmont Park. Before 2010, it was contested on the turf course. There were two forerunners to this race. From 1980 to 1982, a separate stakes event, a two-mile dirt race known as the Kelso Handicap, was held. And in 1984, the Brighton Beach Handicap, a mile-and-a-quarter turf race, was renamed to honor Kelso.

Chapter 10

Damascus: A King Among Giants

Damascus was a racehorse of the highest class, a standout in a time of standouts.[175]

Damascus was voted Horse of the Year and Champion Handicap Horse as a three-year-old after winning most of the major races in his division, including the Woodward Stakes, romping to victory by ten lengths. At four, Damascus won the Brooklyn and also took the Aqueduct and William DuPont Jr. Handicaps, carrying 134 pounds in both races. He was inducted into the Hall of Fame in 1974 and is ranked number sixteen in *Thoroughbred Champions: Top 100 Racehorses of the 20th Century*. He raced during the 1960s—the "true golden age of racing." He came along when fans were in need of a champion in the absence of a Triple Crown winner. Had he raced even just a few years before or after he did, Damascus would have undoubtedly received more respect for his feats. Instead, he rivaled throughout his career with two other stellar handicappers: Dr. Fager and Buckpasser.

Damascus was bred and owned by Mrs. Edith W. Bancroft, daughter of William Woodward Sr., who had owned the historic Maryland horse farm Belair Stud. Her brother, William Woodward Jr., inherited the property after his father's death in 1953, but tragically, just two years later, he was killed at just thirty-five years of age, and the Belair stock was sold at auction. Edith chose to carry on her family's racing tradition—though she did not use Belair as a stable name. Sadly, Mrs. Bancroft began to suffer from Alzheimer's disease around the time of Damascus's birth and was aided by her husband,

Thomas Bancroft Sr., and her mother, Elsie Woodward, both of whom were actively involved in her horse's racing career.

Damascus was foaled on April 14, 1964, at Jonabell Farm in Lexington. A handsome bay, he was named for Damascus steel, which was used for making sword blades; it was also a play off the names of his sire, 1959 Horse of the Year Sword Dancer, and his damsire, Blade of Time.[176] Other sources state that he was named for a Maryland town near his owner's home.[177] Damascus was out of the unraced mare Kerala, who would go on to be Broodmare of the Year in 1967, partly on account of his successes. She was sired by My Babu, champion two-year-old in England and leading sire in the United States. Syndicated for $600,000 in 1955 to Spendthrift Farm, My Babu was the first horse to make a direct flight from Europe to Kentucky, traveling from Ireland in 1956.[178]

Hall of Famer Frank Whiteley Jr.—who conditioned such champions as Tom Rolfe, Ruffian and the mighty Forego in his last two seasons—trained Damascus throughout his three-year racing career. Although Damascus was slow to develop on the track as a two-year-old, he impressed Whiteley, who commented that the colt was "what you'd call a perfect horse around the barn."[179]

Donning Belair's white-and-red polka-dot silks and scarlet cap, which Mrs. Bancroft had inherited from her father, Damascus first went to the post at Aqueduct on September 28, 1966, for a seven-furlong race for maidens. With ten-time leading money-winning jockey and Hall of Famer Bill "Willie" Shoemaker aboard, who rode him in most of his races through his two-and three-year-old seasons, Damascus finished second behind Comprador.

Returning to the same track and racing the same distance two weeks later, he won "easily"[180] by eight lengths. His final two starts of the season came in an allowance at Laurel Park and the one-mile Remsen, and he won them both (the former by twelve lengths). Champion Two-Year-Old honors that year went to the Bold Ruler colt Successor, who defeated the previously unbeaten Florida-bred colt Dr. Fager in the Champagne Stakes. Damascus would rival with Dr. Fager the next two racing seasons.

After wintering in Virginia and South Carolina, Damascus got off to a great start at three with wins in an allowance race at Pimlico, in which he jumped over puddles while racing along and overcame being bumped twice to win by a head, and the Bay Shore Stakes at Aqueduct. In the Gotham Stakes on April 15, he met his match in Dr. Fager. The two co-favorites ran head to head, but in the end it was "the Doctor" in front. Shoemaker blamed himself for the loss and assured Whiteley that Dr. Fager would not defeat Damascus again while he was riding him.[181] He kept his promise.

Next up, in preparation for the Derby, Damascus was entered in the Wood Memorial. His first time going beyond a mile and carrying 126 pounds as the 7–10 favorite, he won by six lengths, defeating Gala Performance and Dawn Glory. On a fast track at the Downs, he managed a third-place finish behind Proud Clarion and Barb's Delight. He had been nervous before the race. As Shoemaker recalled, "Damascus was more rank than he had ever been. Even in the saddling area, or going to the post, he just wasn't himself. And in the race, he took a great deal out of himself in the first half mile or so. By the time we turned for home, he had no finishing kick left."[182]

After the Derby, he was given a companion pony named Duffy and was sent to Laurel to relax away from the press at Pimlico. The final two legs of the Triple Crown were all his. He won the Preakness over In Reality by two and a quarter lengths; Proud Clarion was third. In the Belmont, he "blew by" the Derby winner to defeat Canadian contender Cool Reception by two and a half lengths, running the mile and a half in 2:28⅘.[183] Sadly, the runner-up finished the race with a broken right foreleg and had to be euthanized. The winner's circle was a scene of déjà vu for Shoemaker, who had won the race with Damascus's sire Sword Dancer in 1959. It was also Belair Stud's seventh Belmont Stakes victory.

Sent to Del War, Ron Turcotte replaced Shoemaker in the irons for the Leonard Richards, and Damascus won again. In the William Du Pont Jr. Handicap, he couldn't catch Exceedingly, but he rebounded to win six

Damascus. *Courtesy of the author.*

Damascus in the winner's circle with Bill Shoemaker after winning the Belmont Stakes, June 3, 1967. *Courtesy of the author.*

straight races. In the American Derby, the bay colt set a new track record of 1:46, defeating In Reality and Favorable Turn. He then won the Travers Stakes over Reason to Hail by an astonishing twenty-two lengths, coming from off the pace to equal the track record of 2:01⅗.

In the Aqueduct Stakes, Damascus faced older horses for the first time and, as the 1–5 favorite, defeated Widener Handicap winner Ring Twice, a grandson of Champion Handicapper Stymie, as well as Champion Handicap mare Straight Deal. He ran the mile-and-a-quarter race in a time of 1:48⅕.[184] Under top weight of 128 pounds, Damascus also won the Dwyer.

The biggest race of Damascus's career came on September 30, 1967, in the Woodward Stakes, where "he stood among the mighty and towered over them all."[185] Called the "Race of the Century," it was ranked number thirty-nine in *Horse Racing's Top 100 Moments.* The event brought together three of racing's best horses that season, known as the "Big Three." His old rival Dr. Fager, as well as Buckpasser, a four-year-old son of Tom Fool, joined the bay at Aqueduct. Dr. Fager was coming off wins in the New Hampshire Sweepstakes and Rockingham Special Stakes. Buckpasser had taken both the Metropolitan and Suburban Handicaps earlier in the season and had won the Woodward the year before, en route to claiming Horse of the Year and Champion Three-Year-Old Colt honors. The three-year-olds Damascus and Dr. Fager were both assigned 120 pounds; Buckpasser carried 126.

Buckpasser, like Damascus, liked to come from behind and overtake the leaders in the stretch, whereas Dr. Fager liked to be out front. Knowing this, Whiteley sent out a "rabbit"—a horse that would go to the lead and set fast fractions in the early part of the race—in order to tire Dr. Fager. Champion sprinter Hedevar, who had equaled the world record in winning the previous year's Equipoise Mile, fit the job description, and he did his job well, battling with the front-runner into the stretch while Damascus and Buckpasser stayed back at a slower pace.

Coming from behind as they entered the home stretch, Damascus made "one of the most electrifying moves on the far turn ever witnessed on an American racetrack" to win the race by ten lengths over Buckpasser and Dr. Fager in a time of 2:00⅗. Shoemaker remarked after the race, "This colt gets better all the time, and I'll say it again, though some people don't believe it—Damascus is as good a horse as I have ever ridden. That includes the best, such as Swaps, Kelso, Gallant Man and even Buckpasser himself."[186]

Damascus demonstrated his staying power when he triumphed in the then two-mile Jockey Club Gold Cup, defeating Brooklyn Handicap winner Handsome Boy and Successor. Trying the turf for the first time in the mile-and-a-half D.C. International, he "just failed" to catch that year's champion grass horse Fort Marcy. Both horses were at equal weight of 120 pounds. At year's end, Damascus was crowned Champion Three-Year-Old Colt and Horse of the Year, and he shared Champion Handicap Horse honors with Buckpasser. He also set an earnings record for a single season with $817,941, which stood until Secretariat beat it in 1973.[187] In the words of turf writer Charles Hatton in the *American Racing Manual*:

> [Damascus] *danced all the dances and ran all the distances from a mile to two miles. Never did we see him spit out the bit…and he was confronted with such defiant tasks as carrying topweight of 128 pounds in the Dwyer, giving Ring Twice and Straight Deal actual weight in the*

> *Aqueduct, and running smooth-shod in unaccustomed going in the grassy Laurel International. Fort Marcy won the money that day, but Damascus won the crowd's heart.*[188]

Damascus was assigned top weight of 133 pounds on the Blood-Horse Free Handicap. As a four-year-old, he spent the winter at Santa Anita, winning the Malibu and San Fernando Stakes, and then finished second in the Charles H. Strub Stakes on a sloppy track behind Most Host, to whom he conceded 12 pounds. At this time, jockey Manny Ycaza replaced Shoemaker, who was laid up with an injury due to a nasty fall. In the Suburban, Damascus was assigned 133 pounds, a significant jump from the 128 he had carried in the Dwyer the year before. Dr. Fager, carrying 132 pounds, got the better of him again, and Damascus also failed to catch Bold Hour (113), finishing third. The final time of 1:59⅗ equaled the track record.

After a repeat performance in the Haskell, in which he was beaten by Bold Hour and Mr. Right, conceding weight to both, Damascus then returned to top form to avenge his loss to Dr. Fager in the Brooklyn, setting a new track record of 1:59⅕ for a mile and a quarter and breaking the record set by Dr. Fager when he defeated Damascus in the Suburban just a few weeks prior.[189] With that victory, he surpassed the million-dollar mark in earnings, becoming racing's eighth millionaire Thoroughbred.[190]

In both the William Du Pont and Aqueduct Handicaps, Damascus carried 134 pounds to victory. The Arkansas-bred Nodouble, who would go on to earn Champion Handicap honors in 1969 and 1970, defeated him in the Michigan Mile and One-Eighth Handicap. Damascus could not repeat in the Woodward, finishing second to Mr. Right. In the final start of his career—the Jockey Club Gold Cup—he bowed a tendon and came in last place, the only time he finished out of the money. In a total of thirty-two starts, he won twenty-one times. His career earnings totaled $1,176,781.

Damascus was retired to stud at Claiborne Farm, where he sired seventy-one stakes winners and was a successful broodmare sire. His sons included Canadian Champion Two-Year-Old Lord Durham; American stakes winners Honorable Miss, Highland Blade and Timeless Moment; Private Account, sire of undefeated mare Personal Ensign; millionaire Desert Wine; and the Irish champion Belted Earl. His daughters produced over one hundred stakes winners, including Shadeed and Capades. Damascus died in his paddock at age thirty-one on August 8, 1995. The Damascus Stakes is a seven-furlong race for three-year-olds run each November at Santa Anita Park.

Chapter 11

Forego: The Last Great Weight Carrier

There was no such thing as "too much weight" for Forego, and race fans loved him and owner Martha Gerry for taking that notion to the limit. "A horse is supposed to carry weight and try to beat the best," said Mrs. Gerry. "That's why they call it handicap racing."[191]

Known as the "Freight Train," the old racetrack saying "weight will stop a freight train" simply didn't apply to Forego, the top handicap horse of the 1970s and the last of the great weight carriers. He set a track record in the Brooklyn Handicap (which he won three times), carrying 132 pounds, and won four consecutive runnings of the Woodward Stakes. Under an impost of 137 pounds, he defeated Honest Pleasure in the Marlboro Cup as a six-year-old. The race was ranked number twenty-six in *Horse Racing's Top 100 Moments.* The gelding raced a total of twenty-four times carrying 130 pounds or more and won thirteen of those races, finishing out of the money on only three occasions. Forego won eight Eclipse Awards—including three consecutive Horse of the Year titles and four Champion Older Male titles—and was inducted into the Hall of Fame in 1979. In the *Blood-Horse*'s ranking of the top one hundred racehorses of the twentieth century, he is ranked eighth.

Forego was owned and bred by Mrs. Martha Gerry, who managed Lazy F Ranch near Houston, Texas. Martha's father, William Stamps Farish, was one of the founders of Humble Oil Company and became involved in racing later in his life. Sadly, he died of a heart attack just after buying four fillies at the Saratoga yearling sale in 1942. Martha, at age twenty-four, along with her husband, Edward H. Gerry, whose family has also been involved in the industry, took over the management of his horses. Edward's father, Robert, had owned horses at his Aknutsi Stud in Delhi, New York, since 1920. He was reportedly the underbidder for Man o' War when he was sold at the Saratoga yearling sale in 1918, and his horse Audacious defeated Exterminator in the 1921 Suburban.[192]

Born at Claiborne Farm on May 1, 1970, Forego was sired by the undefeated classic Argentinian winner Forli, in whom Mrs. Gerry had a couple shares, and out of one-time stakes winner Lady Golconda, a daughter of Champion Two-Year-Old Colt and Preakness winner Hasty Road (a maternal grandson of Discovery). He was named by merging the beginning letters of the names of his sire and dam; Mrs. Gerry added the "e" so that it changed the meaning of the name from "to do without" to "to precede or go before in place or time."[193] One wonders if the horse may have had a different fate otherwise.

Sherrill Ward and Frank Y. Whiteley Jr. were Forego's principal trainers throughout his five-year racing career. Ward had previously conditioned Summer Tan, archrival of Horse of the Year Nashua, as well as Idun, champion filly in 1957 and 1958. He trained Forego for his first three seasons.

Forego overcame significant leg troubles to get to the winner's circle. First, he had an enlarged outside sesamoid in his left front foot. Sesamoids are two small bones located above and behind the fetlock joint on a horse's lower leg. He also frequently suffered from wind puffs (a buildup of synovial fluid) in his right front leg and was prone to injury on the racetrack. Whiteley reportedly spent three hours every day hosing down the horse's legs with cold water and rubbing them down.[194]

Slow to mature, Forego was gelded, partly on account of his temperament, but he eventually grew to a height of 17.1hh. He was sent to the Lexington farm of Ward's brother, John T. Ward, to be broken to saddle and begin his training for the track.

Unraced at two, Forego was outfitted with steel shoes on his hind feet at three to prevent the feet from spreading.[195] He still managed to win nine races out of eighteen starts that season. His regular rider was Pete Anderson, who was replaced by Heliodoro Gustines when Anderson had trouble making weight. In his first race—a seven-furlong sprint for maidens at Hialeah—the gelding finished fourth after being bumped. Less than two weeks later, he won a six-furlong race by eight lengths. After an impressive allowance win at the same distance, Ward sent him out in stakes company, entering him in the Hutcheson

Stakes at Gulfstream Park in Hallandale Beach, Florida. He finished second but rebounded to win an allowance. Then it was time to prep for the Derby.

Forego finished second in the Florida Derby, behind Royal and Regal, and then lost to My Gallant, running fifth as the 5–2 favorite in the Blue Grass Stakes at Keeneland. He finished fourth behind Secretariat in the Kentucky Derby after hitting the rail when switching leads in the stretch. He returned to the barn with white paint marks along his left side.[196] Ron Turcotte, Big Red's jockey, recalled that Forego "...amazed me the first time I saw him in Florida. He was a big animal. Watching him run, it was unbelievable."[197]

On Belmont Stakes day, Forego won a mile-and-a-sixteenth allowance race by nine lengths in a time of 1:40⅘, just off the track record. Secretariat's owner, Penny Tweedy, was impressed with the performance and congratulated Mrs. Gerry, remarking, "What a terrific race. What a fine horse."[198] Later that day, Secretariat broke the Belmont Stakes record, and Forego was all but forgotten.

Sportswriter William Leggett observed that bad timing was a problem with Forego, as he was overshadowed by other top racehorses and major sporting events for much of his three-, four- and five-year-old seasons.[199] On the day he won the Roamer Handicap, November 25, 1973, Ohio State and Michigan played to a tie, resulting in a vote to determine which team would go to the Rose Bowl. On the same day that Forego won the 1974 Widener Handicap, UCLA was bumped from the NCAA basketball finals for the first time in eight years. His Carter victory occurred just ten minutes before long shot Little Current won the Preakness. Nolan Ryan pitched a no-hitter on the day Forego won the Woodward. In November, while he cantered home in the Jockey Club Gold Cup, Michigan State beat Ohio State—one of college football's biggest upsets. In 1975, the gelding's second Carter win occurred on the same day that Master Derby defeated Foolish Pleasure in the Preakness. His Brooklyn win received hardly any notice due to Billie Jean King's win at Wimbledon and an event that will live in horse racing infamy: Ruffian's breakdown in a match race against Foolish Pleasure. Eventually, Forego's feats on the racetrack were too great to be ignored.

The 1970s were a turning point for handicap racing. Forego could hardly escape ever-increasing weight assignments as he stacked up win after win, and with a shortage of weight-for-age events, handicaps were really the only option for much of the racing season. As Alfred G. Vanderbilt II remarked:

> *There used to be jockeys around who could make 100 pounds or even into the 90s. I hear all the time that there just aren't enough riders around today*

> *who can get that low and, therefore, the weights must stay up. I think it should be the responsibility of the trainers to find such riders. Also, Forego has to start out his year in the handicaps, and if he wins, his weights necessarily go up. There just aren't enough weight-for-age races left, and the few that are come up in the fall.*[200]

In the summer of 1973, Ward had to have open-heart surgery, and so Eddie Hayward, a former jockey who had conditioned Kentucky Derby winner Dark Star, took over training duties for Forego's remaining races of the season. The bay gelding ran third in the Withers Stakes and was second in the Jerome. In the fall, he won his first stakes race, the Roamer Handicap, in the stakes record time of 1:54⅗ and at top weight of 123 pounds, defeating My Gallant and Twice a Prince. On December 8, in the Discovery Handicap at Aqueduct under 127 pounds—the highest impost ever assigned in the race—Forego won by three-quarters of a length as the 3–5 favorite and was just a fifth of a second behind the track record set by Riva Ridge under 130 pounds. He ended the season having earned $188,909, the leader in stakes earnings. He was co-rated with Sham at 127 pounds on the Blood-Horse Free Handicap, second only to Secretariat at 136.

At four, Forego demonstrated his versatility, winning eight races ranging from seven furlongs to two miles. On February 9, he carried 125 pounds in the Donn Handicap and won by a nose over True Knight despite having cut his right hip in the van ride over from Hialeah, where he had been training for the race. He went on to defeat his five-year-old rival twice more, in the Gulfstream Park and Widener Handicaps. In the Gulfstream, Forego carried 127 pounds, and racing secretary Eddie McKinsey defended his assignment by paying the gelding great respect, saying, "Right now, I rate Forego the best handicap horse in the country."[201] Ward, meanwhile, was not happy with the weight assignment and, in fact, was unsure of whether or not to send him to the post. Sent off as the second choice in the betting at 7–5, he won the race by half a length. Thrilled, Ward commented, "I expected him to run big, but he ran even bigger than I thought he would. What really pleases me is that he proved he has heart. I always knew he had speed. Now I know that he will fight back when he's challenged."[202]

Next it was off to New York, where Forego carried 129 pounds to victory as the 7–5 favorite in the seven-furlong Carter, defeating record-breaking sprinter and eventual top sire Mr. Prospector. This performance turned heads. In the Met Mile, he was assigned 134 pounds—the heaviest impost assigned for the race and last carried by winner Devil Diver in

Forego with Heliodoro Gustines up after winning the Gulfstream Park Handicap on February 23, 1974. *Courtesy of the* Thoroughbred Times/*Keeneland*.

1944—and finished second behind long shot Arbees Boy, to whom he conceded 22 pounds. It was around this time that Gustines began to ride Forego strategically, being careful to win by as little a margin as possible to avoid heavier weight assignments in future races.[203]

Second again in the Nassau County Handicap, Forego then won the Brooklyn in a time of 1:54⅘ for the mile and three-sixteenths. In the Suburban, Forego carried 131 pounds and finished third behind True Knight and Plunk. He was third in the Marlboro on a sloppy track but came back to win the mile-and-a-half Woodward, at that time a weight-for-age event, under 126 pounds. He carried 131 pounds to victory in the seven-furlong Vosburgh, and in November, he won the two-mile weight-for-age Jockey Club Gold Cup by two and a half lengths under 124 pounds at odds of 3–5. All three victories occurred in the short span of five weeks, and he became the first horse to win all three races in the same year.[204]

Forego ended the season with eight wins, two seconds, two thirds and a fourth-place finish in thirteen races, earning $545,086.[205] At year's end, he was voted Horse of the Year, Champion Sprinter and Champion Older Male. He was the first horse in history to win the Gold Cup and be voted Champion Sprinter in the same year. Mrs. Gerry received the New York Turf Writer's Association award as the woman who did the most for racing.

At five, Forego started the season in Florida, winning the Seminole Handicap and his second Widener. He carried 131 pounds in the latter—the most weight carried to victory in the race. In New York, he won the Carter under 134 pounds. Only Tom Fool and Bold Ruler won carrying more, at 135 pounds. Running head to head with Stop the Music, Forego won by a head in a time of 1:21⅗, beating his own time in the race the year before. He then ran third in the Metropolitan behind Gold and Myrrh and Stop the Music, carrying 136 pounds to the winner's 121, but won the second and third races of the New York Handicap Triple in spectacular fashion.

In the Brooklyn, sporting bandages on his hind legs, Forego won in a time of 1:59⅘ under 132 pounds, conceding 23 pounds to runner-up Monetary Principle and smashing Whisk Broom II's questionable record of 2:00 for the race. The Suburban was lengthened from a mile and a quarter to a mile and a half in 1975, but Forego still got up to win by a head under 134 pounds. He made history by becoming the first horse to win a major race in the United States at that distance carrying that much weight.[206]

Forego was fourth in the Governor's Stakes, in which he carried top weight of 134 pounds. He gave 19 pounds to winner three-year-old champion Wajima, a son of Bold Ruler, and 9 pounds to runner-up and Kentucky Derby winner Foolish Pleasure. Wajima beat him again, this time just narrowly, in the Marlboro Cup, carrying 119 pounds to Forego's 129. But the gelding evened the score with a two-length victory in the Woodward. The weight spread was 7 pounds, with Forego carrying 126 pounds.

Although he was entered in the Jockey Club Gold Cup, Forego was scratched after pulling a suspensory ligament and ended the season with six wins in nine starts. In Ward's statement to the media, he announced his retirement from training due to increased pain from arthritis. Forego ended his five-year-old season with six wins, one second, one third and a fourth-place finish. He moved to John T. Ward's farm in Lexington to take some time off. He was once again crowned Horse of the Year—only the fourth horse to win two titles in a row—as well as Champion Older Male.

In his six-year-old season, Frank Whiteley Jr., with the assistance of his son, David, took over Forego's training. The horse's first start came in an allowance race at Belmont, which he won handily under 126 pounds. In the Met Mile, he carried 130 pounds and defeated 1975 Preakness winner Master Derby. He won the Nassau County under 132 pounds with Jacinto Vasquez aboard and then lost a photo finish to Foolish Pleasure in the Suburban, which was held before the Brooklyn and was shortened that year to a mile and three-sixteenths.[207] He carried 134 pounds and conceded 9 to the winner. After the race, Whiteley remarked, "We got beat a tough one, but that's part of handicap racing. If your horse is good, you pick up weight."[208]

Forego next took the Brooklyn—his third—under the same weight, defeating Lord Rebeau and Foolish Pleasure. After a third-place finish in the Haskell, the gelding won his third Woodward, this time under handicap conditions and at a distance of a mile and one-eighth. He ran the race in a time of 1:45⅘, just ⅖ of a second off the track record set by Secretariat in 1973 under 124 pounds,[209] and he did it carrying 135 pounds (including new rider Bill Shoemaker), conceding 20 pounds to runner-up Dance Spell.

Two weeks later, Forego was assigned 137 pounds for the Marlboro Handicap, the second-highest weight in Belmont Park's history. It rained on the day of the race, and Tommy Trotter, the secretary at Belmont Park, worried that the horse might hurt himself and that racing fans would hold him responsible. Nonetheless, Forego went to the post and performed a near-impossible feat. He moved up from fifth place to pass the leader, Travers winner Honest Pleasure, in the stretch and won the race by a head—just short of the track record. Of the race, Shoemaker recalled:

> *When we were nearing the top of the stretch with a little more than a quarter of a mile to run, I didn't think Forego would be in the money. I knew darn well I wasn't going to win. Then he dug in and started to roll. With an eighth of a mile left it still seemed impossible. At the sixteenth pole, I thought, "Hey, just maybe he can get there." When he did, I was amazed. Forego is the greatest horse I have ever ridden.*[210]

The *Daily Racing Form* assigned Forego a record 140 pounds on the Free Handicap for older males. When the votes were cast for the Eclipse Awards, Forego was declared Horse of the Year for a third consecutive year.

At seven, the mighty gelding won four races in seven starts, including his fourth Woodward (under 133 pounds), second Metropolitan (133 pounds) and Nassau County Handicap (136), and ran second in two: the Suburban, in which he carried 138 pounds and lost by a neck to Quiet Little Table, and the Brooklyn, in which he carried 137 pounds and was almost twelve lengths behind Great Contractor at the wire. In the latter, Forego deviated from his typical running style; instead of sitting off the pace and waiting to fire in the stretch, Shoemaker took him to the lead after a half mile due to a slow early pace, but the horse was unable to maintain it for the final quarter mile.[211] In the Whitney, carrying 136, he finished in last place on a muddy track. *Sports Illustrated* reported that it was "A Race He Should Have Foregone."[212] He earned $267,740 for the year and was voted Champion Older Male for the third time.

In 1978, Forego ran twice. He won a seven-furlong allowance, defeating top sprinter Dr. Patches, and then finished fifth in the Suburban. It was decided to finally retire him after calcium deposits were found on his sesamoids. He had won a total of thirty-four races (twenty-four of them stakes) in fifty-seven starts, and his career earnings were just shy of $2 million. That September, he led the post parade for the Marlboro Cup, in which Triple Crown winners Affirmed and Seattle Slew met for the first time.

Forego was initially retired to John Ward's farm near Keeneland, where he would gallop around his pasture whenever he heard the roar of the crowd at the nearby track.[213] In 1981, Forego moved to the Hall of Champions at the Kentucky Horse Park, where he lived until his death in 1997. He was euthanized after fracturing his right hind pastern bone in his paddock. He is buried at the park. His epitaph on his gravestone reads, "A towering champion, he had the speed at win at seven furlongs. The staying power to win at two miles. The strength to carry greater weight than all rivals and triumph with brilliance."

The Forego Stakes, formerly a handicap, is a seven-furlong Grade I race for three-year-olds and up, held each year at Saratoga Racetrack. Inaugurated in 1980, the event was held at Belmont Park until 1984 and originally contested at a mile. From 1982 to 1999, it was raced at seven furlongs and from 2000 to 2002 at six and a half furlongs.

Chapter 12
THE END OF AN ERA

To speak of "classic" handicaps is deliberately to produce a contradiction in terms, because a "classic" is designed to test for superiority at even terms, while a handicap is an intentional attempt to destroy superiority by weight. The ideal of the "classic" is for the best horse to win; the intent of a handicap is to see that he does not, or at least, that he wins no more frequently than inferior horses. In American racing, the handicap, originally planned for second-flight horses, has become the staple of racing for 4-year-olds and up, and the stakes for older horses, at weight-for-age without allowances, may be counted on the fingers of one hand, even if one has lost a finger or two.

It must be confessed, though, that a handicap tells something which a classic does not. The classic picks out the best horse; the handicap measures the margin of superiority over his contemporaries. The classic winner can sweep the boards at 126 pounds. Can he do it at 128? At 130? At 132? At 134? Somewhere along the line we find his limitation, we measure with some accuracy, in the old phrase, "how good he is."[214]

How things have changed in the sixty-eight years since Joe Palmer made clear the purpose of the handicap and its distinction from the "classic" horse race. In fact, it could be said that the situation has been completely reversed.

In the late 1950s, stallion syndications started to become popular, and for owners, retiring top sire prospects became more appealing than risking defeat and injury on the track. At this time, weight carrying was a controversial topic. Opinions varied even among those who worked together. In 1956,

Robert Kleberg, then owner of King Ranch, commented on weight carrying in an article for *Sports Illustrated*: "There's no question that horses are capable of carrying a lot more weight. But my point is that I can't see the necessity for requiring them to do so at the risk of breaking them down."[215]

Kleberg made a valid point. While Whisk Broom II may have won the Suburban under 139 pounds, he went lame shortly after the race and was retired. Roseben, Exterminator, Devil Diver, Kelso, Damascus and Forego all eventually reached their limit and broke, paying for their greatness in the form of injury and defeat. Others, such as Tom Fool, ran away from impossible weights and were retired to avoid irreparable damage.

Max Hirsch, trainer for King Ranch, viewed handicaps in a different light:

> *If great horses in the past could win carrying more than 130 pounds, a great horse should be able to do the same thing today—if he's a great horse. Everybody appreciates the fact that a horse isn't going to win every race. Owners shouldn't expect to win everything. They should be satisfied to run with any weight assigned by a competent Racing Secretary, and be thankful when they win that their horse is good enough to do the job…I like to think of racing as a sport even if it's also a business. Nobody forces a man to enter his horse in any race, but once he decides to run, then run for the pleasure of it and forget about how much money your horse might win you. Weight is going to get you beaten once in a while, but a man who doesn't expect to take a beating shouldn't be in horse racing to start with.*[216]

"No one stays at the top forever," as the saying goes, and heavy weight handicaps continued for several more decades even though their popularity with owners and trainers waned. In 1971, the awarding of "Champion Handicap Male" honors became part of the Eclipse Awards program. The title was changed, along with the award criteria, making only horses four years of age or older eligible for "American Champion Older Male Horse" honors.

Things changed again in the 1980s when purses increased with the introduction of the Breeder's Cup. And so racing again began to see more horses racing past the age of three but carrying lesser weights.

On August 30, 1998, Florida-bred Skip Away—a great-grandson of Damascus—carried 131 pounds en route to victory in the Philip H. Iselin Handicap at Monmouth Park. He conceded 18 pounds to his nearest rival, Stormin Fever. No horse has been assigned 130 pounds in a major route race in the United States since then. Curlin and Wise Dan are the only Champion

Older Male horses since that time to have won carrying more than 124 pounds in a handicap. In 2008, Curlin carried 128 pounds to victory in the Stephen Foster, conceding between 10 and 15 pounds to the other starters. Wise Dan won carrying as much as 129 pounds as a six-year-old.

Until the late 1990s, handicaps were much more common, while there were fewer stakes races than there are today. As racing entered a new millennium, the number of Grade I events increased as the number of handicaps began to decrease. Top weight assignments and weight spread (how much the top horse must concede) also declined. Between 1970 and 2008, top weight averages in Grade I handicaps dropped by three pounds, and the spread decreased by almost thirteen pounds.[217]

Today, the remaining Grade I handicaps are almost entirely exclusive to New York and California, with a few still being run in Florida, Kentucky and Arkansas. According to Ryan Goldberg of the *Daily Racing Form*, only five true Grade I route races remain: the Donn, Santa Anita, Stephen Foster, Hollywood Gold Cup and Whitney. Many of the former top handicaps, including the Brooklyn and Suburban, have been downgraded and the purses dropped. Many more of the great handicaps have disappeared completely. Keeneland no longer has graded stakes handicaps, and the big tracks have changed their handicaps to allowance or weight-for-age events.[218] Handicaps with real weights appear to have become a thing of the past. Turf writer Gary West has gone so far as to proclaim that "modern handicaps are largely a sham."[219]

While racing secretaries once had the upper hand, so to speak, trainers now hold the cards in terms of choosing the best race and, in most cases, the weight assignment for their horses. With ample stakes races to choose from and fewer offerings of "true" handicaps, trainers can easily avoid high weight assignments. Whereas racing was once about sportsmanship and the fans, much of the industry's operations are now managed primarily from a financial standpoint. It is important to note, however, that owners and trainers are now in a position where they can do what's best for their horses, and many use this justification when backing out of races with heavier weight assignments.

Others see possible defeat under heavier weight as costing the sport by denying its great champions victories they deserve. In the words of trainer Carl Nafzger, "[No] Grade I should have weights. That only hurts a great horse…and only diminishes the fact that somebody else beats him. This really destroys racing. The fans don't understand it, and it's idiotic that we can't have a Grade I series that's weight for age. We're the only sport in the world that just has to destroy its champions. Destroy is the word."[220]

Some, however, still see handicap conditions as a way for good horses to prove their greatness. As trainer Nick Zito explains, "…that's what makes a champion, to overcome this obstacle."[221]

There are a number of factors that point to the diminishing popularity of handicaps. The focus has shifted over the past few decades to two- and three-year-olds, with more money dedicated to stakes purses. There is also more incentive for top colts to retire to the breeding shed after far fewer victories than in the past, as more money can be made in the breeding business. The opposite was true for horses such as Discovery and Equipoise, who, at four years of age, could earn five times as much in purses than in stud fees.[222] Few champion colts today continue their racing careers past the age of three; in fact, only two, Tiznow and Animal Kingdom, have done so since 1998.

The introduction of the Breeder's Cup is also partially responsible, as it changed the criteria for how races qualify for funding and how horses may accrue points so as to be nominated for the championship races. It is believed that handicaps deter top horses because of the increased weights; the point behind the championships is to encourage a face-off between the best horses in each division.[223]

Another reason handicaps have been dropped from racing calendars is because of the higher weight allowance for jockeys. While it was not uncommon for jockeys to ride at or below 110 pounds back in the heyday of racing, starting allowances at most tracks today are much higher. Few top jockeys ride at less than 115 pounds, and racing secretaries have not lifted the top of the scale to adjust for these changes.[224]

Interestingly, it is the top fillies and mares that stay in training longer than the males that are now being asked to carry more weight. Three-time champion older female Azeri carried as much as 128 pounds, frequently conceding weight to her rivals; Sprinter Xtra Heat carried 127 across the finish line in the 2002 Vagrancy; and Zenyatta won under 129 pounds in the 2009 Vanity Handicap.

Of course, many of racing's leading ladies have carried excessive weights on American racetracks. Pan Zareta, a Texas-bred known as "Queen of the Turf," frequently raced against males and once won under an astonishing 146 pounds, conceding 46 pounds to the runner-up. Regret, the first filly to win the Derby against the colts in 1915, won under 129 pounds as a five-year-old in the Gazelle Handicap. Oklahoma-bred Lady's Secret, daughter of Secretariat, carried the same weight to victory in the 1986 Ruffian Handicap. Florida-bred Ta Wee, champion sprinter in 1969 and 1970, won the Interborough Handicap under 142 pounds.

Are handicaps doomed to become a thing of the past? While many say yes, others argue that they may be making a comeback. On June 29, 2013, Wise Dan broke a weight record when he carried 128 pounds to victory in the Grade II Firecracker Handicap, a one-mile race on turf at Churchill Downs. The previous record was 124 pounds, carried by winner Kitten's Joy in 2005. In the Grade I Hollywood Gold Cup on July 6, winner Game on Dude carried 127 pounds, the most weight carried by a winner of the race since 1982.

On August 10, Wise Dan won his second consecutive Fourstardave Handicap, a Grade II event, carrying 129 pounds and conceding 12 pounds to runner-up King Kreesa. Charlie LoPresti, trainer of the chestnut who earned 2012 and 2013 Horse of the Year honors, agreed with the weight assignment, saying, "To prove that he's a great horse, like everybody's talking about, he had to carry that weight."[225] LoPresti has gained the respect of horsemen and racing fans for just that attitude. Only time will tell if Wise Dan or another horse of equal talent and ability will be asked to carry top weight of 130 pounds.

Although we may not again see such great weight carriers as those of the past century, there is reason to hope that equally celebrated champions may be crowned as we proceed through a new, albeit challenging, era for horse racing. Perhaps we will see new types of races and divisions created and new criteria set to measure the courage and fortitude of our equine athletes that will test the sport to new levels of sustainability. Of course, there are numerous ways of determining greatness on the racetrack—winning under weight is merely one of them. How we will quantify a horse's greatness and measure "how good he is" in the absence of handicaps, however, remains to be seen.

Appendix A

Champion Handicap Male Horse Winners, 1900–70

Year	Horse	Age	Trainer	Owner	State/ Country Bred
1900	Kinley Mack	4	Peter Wimmer	Eastin & Larable	Unknown
1901	Banastar	6	Charles F. Hill	Clarence H. Mackay	Unknown
1902	Gold Heels	4	Matthew M. Allen	F.C. McLewee and Diamond Jim Brady	PA
1903	Waterboy	4	A. Jack Joyner	James Ben Ali Haggin	Unknown
1903	Hermis	4	William Shields	Edward R. Thomas	KY
1904	Hermis	5	William Shields	Edward R. Thomas	KY
1905	Delhi	4	James G. Rowe, Sr.	James R. Keene	Unknown
1905	Ort Wells	4	Enoch Wishard	John A. Drake	Unknown
1906	Go Between	5	William Shields	Edward R. Thomas	Unknown
1907	Nealon	4	Frank M. Taylor	Charles E. Durnell	Unknown
1908	Ballot	5	James G. Rowe Sr.	James R. Keene	KY
1909	King James	4	Sam Hildreth	Sam Hildreth	KY
1910	Ballot	6	James G. Rowe Sr.	James R. Keene	KY
1910	Fitz Herbert	4	Sam Hildreth	Charles Kohler	Unknown
1911	Plate Glass	5	Jake Byer	Philip S.P. Randolph	Unknown
1912	Star Charter	4	John F. Schorr	John W. Schorr	Unknown
1913	Whisk Broom II	6	James G. Rowe Sr.	Harry Payne Whitney	KY

Appendix A

Year	Horse	Age	Trainer	Owner	State/ Country Bred
1914	Borrow	6	James G. Rowe Sr.	Harry Payne Whitney	KY
1914	Great Britain	4	J. Walters	George M. Hendrie	KY
1915	Roamer	4	A. Jack Goldsborough	Andrew Miller	KY
1916	Short Grass	8	Unknown	Emil Hertz	IRE
1916	Roamer	5	A. Jack Goldsborough	Andrew Miller	KY
1917	Old Rosebud	6	Frank D. Weir	Frank D. Weir & Hamilton Applegate	KY
1918	Cudgel	4	H. Guy Bedwell	J.K.L. Ross	NJ
1919	Sun Briar	4	Henry McDaniel	Willis Sharpe Kilmer	KY
1919	Cudgel	5	H. Guy Bedwell	J.K.L. Ross	NJ
1920	Exterminator	5	Henry McDaniel	Willis Sharpe Kilmer	KY
1921	Mad Hatter	5	Sam Hildreth	Harry F. Sinclair	KY
1921	Exterminator	6	Willie Knapp	Willis Sharpe Kilmer	KY
1922	Grey Lag	4	Sam Hildreth	Harry F. Sinclair	KY
1922	Exterminator	7	Eugene Wayland	Willis Sharpe Kilmer	KY
1923	Grey Lag	5	Sam Hildreth	Harry F. Sinclair	KY
1924	Epinard	4	H. Eugene Leigh	Pierre Wertheimer	FR
1925	Sarazan	4	Max Hirsch	Virginia Fair Vanderbilt	KY
1926	Sarazan	5	Max Hirsch	Virginia Fair Vanderbilt	KY
1927	Chance Play	4	John I. Smith	Log Cabin Stable	NY
1928	Mike Hall	4	Walter W. Taylor	Hal Price Headley	Unknown
1929	Diavolo	4	James E. Fitzsimmons	Wheatley Stable	Unknown
1929	Sun Beau	4	Andrew G. Blakely	Willis Sharpe Kilmer	VA
1930	Blue Larkspur	4	Henry J. Thompson	Edward R. Bradley	KY

Appendix A

Year	Horse	Age	Trainer	Owner	State/ Country Bred
1930	Sun Beau	5	W.S. Crawford	Willis Sharpe Kilmer	VA
1931	Sun Beau	6	Andy Schuttinger	Willis Sharpe Kilmer	VA
1932	Equipoise	4	Thomas J. Healey	C.V. Whitney	KY
1933	Equipoise	5	Thomas J. Healey	C.V. Whitney	KY
1934	Equipoise	6	Thomas J. Healey	C.V. Whitney	KY
1935	Discovery	4	Bud Stotler	Alfred G. Vanderbilt II	KY
1936	Discovery	5	Bud Stotler	Alfred G. Vanderbilt II	KY
1937	Seabiscuit	4	Tom Smith	Charles S. Howard	KY
1938	Seabiscuit	5	Tom Smith	Charles S. Howard	KY
1939	Kayak II	4	Horatio Luro	Charles S. Howard	ARG
1940	Challedon	4	Louis Schaefer	William L. Brann	MD
1941	Big Pebble (TSD)	5	William B. Finnegan	Edward S. Moore	KY
1941	Mioland (DRF)	4	Tom Smith	Charles S. Howard	OR
1942	Whirlaway	4	Ben A. Jones	Calumet Farm	KY
1943	Devil Diver (DRF)	4	John M. Gaver Sr.	Helen Hay Whitney	KY
1943	Market Wise (TSD)	5	George W. Carroll	Louis Tufano	VA
1944	Devil Diver	5	John M. Gaver Sr.	Helen Hay Whitney	KY
1945	Stymie	4	Hirsch Jacobs	Ethel D. Jacobs	TX
1946	Armed	5	Ben A. Jones	Calumet Farm	KY
1947	Armed	6	Ben A. Jones	Calumet Farm	KY
1948	Shannon II (TSD)	7	William Molter	Neil S. McCarthy	AUS
1948	Citation (DRF)	3	Ben A. Jones	Calumet Farm	KY
1949	Coaltown	4	Ben A. Jones	Calumet Farm	KY
1950	Noor	5	Burley Parke	Charles S. Howard	GB
1951	Citation (TSD)	6	Ben A. Jones	Calumet Farm	KY
1951	Hill Prince (DRF)	4	Casey Hayes	Christopher Chenery	VA
1952	Crafty Admiral	4	Robert T. Odom	Charfran Stable	KY
1953	Tom Fool	4	Duval A. Headley	Greentree Stables	KY

Year	Horse	Age	Trainer	Owner	State/ Country Bred
1954	Native Dancer	4	William C. Winfrey	Alfred G. Vanderbilt II	KY
1955	High Gun	4	Max Hirsch	King Ranch	KY
1956	Swaps	4	Mesh Tenney	Rex C. Ellsworth	CA
1957	Dedicate	5	G. Carey Winfrey	Jan Winfrey Burke	KY
1958	Round Table	4	William Molter	Kerr Stable	KY
1959	Round Table (TRA)	5	William Molter	Kerr Stable	KY
1959	Sword Dancer (DRF)	3	J. Elliott Burch	Brookmeade Stable	VA
1960	Bald Eagle	5	Woody Stephens	Cain Hoy Stable	KY
1961	Kelso	4	Carl Hanford	Bohemia Stable	KY
1962	Kelso	5	Carl Hanford	Bohemia Stable	KY
1963	Kelso	6	Carl Hanford	Bohemia Stable	KY
1964	Kelso	7	Carl Hanford	Bohemia Stable	KY
1965	Roman Brother	4	Burley Parke	Harbor View Farm	FL
1966	Bold Bidder (TRA)	4	Woody Stephens	John R. Gaines	KY
1966	Buckpasser (DRF)	3	Edward A. Neloy	Ogden Phipps	KY
1967	Buckpasser (TRA) (TSD)	4	Edward A. Neloy	Ogden Phipps	KY
1967	Damascus (DRF)	3	Frank Y. Whitely	Edith W. Bancroft	KY
1968	Dr. Fager	4	John A. Nerud	William L. McKnight	FL
1969	Nodouble (TRA)	4	J. Bert Sonnier	Gene Goff	AR
1969	Arts and Letters (DRF)	3	J. Elliott Burch	Rokeby Stable	VA
1970	Nodouble (TRA)	5	J. Bert Sonnier	Gene Goff	AR
1970	Fort Marcy (DRF)	6	J. Elliott Burch	Rokeby Stable	VA

DRF = Daily Racing Form champion

TSD = *Turf and Sports Digest* champion

TRA = Thoroughbred Racing Associations champion

Appendix B

Champion Older Male Horse Eclipse Award Winners, 1971–2013

Year	Horse	Age	Trainer	Owner	State/ Country Bred
1971	Ack Ack	5	Charlie Whittingham	Buddy Fogeison	KY
1972	Autobiography	4	Pancho Martin	Sigmund Sommer	KY
1973	Riva Ridge	4	Lucien Laurin	Estate of C.T. Chenery	KY
1974	Forego	4	Frank Y. Whitely Jr.	Lazy F Ranch	KY
1975	Forego	5	Frank Y. Whitely Jr.	Lazy F Ranch	KY
1976	Forego	6	Frank Y. Whitely Jr.	Lazy F Ranch	KY
1977	Forego	7	Frank Y. Whitely Jr.	Lazy F Ranch	KY
1978	Seattle Slew	4	Douglas R. Peterson	K. & M. Taylor/J. & S. Hill	KY
1979	Affirmed	4	Laz Barrera	Harbor View Farm	FL
1980	Spectacular Bid	4	Bud Delp	Harksworth Farm	KY
1981	John Henry	6	Ron McAnally	Dotsam Stable	KY
1982	Lemhi Gold	4	Laz Barrera	Aaron U. Jones	KY
1983	Bates Motel	4	John H.M. Gosden	Jacqueline Phillips and Michael Riordan	KY
1984	Slew O' Gold	4	John O. Hertler	Equusequity Stable	KY
1985	Vanlandingham	4	Claude R. McGaughey III	Loblolly Stable	KY
1986	Turkoman	4	Gary F. Jones	Corbin J. Robinson	KY

Year	Horse	Age	Trainer	Owner	State/ Country Bred
1987	Ferdinand	4	Charlie Whittingham	Elizabeth A. Keck	KY
1988	Alysheba	4	Jack Van Berg	Dorothy and Pamela Scharbauer	KY
1989	Blushing John	4	Richard J. Lundy	Allen E. Paulson	KY
1990	Criminal Type	5	D. Wayne Lukas	Calumet and Jurgen K. Arnemann	KY
1991	Black Tie Affair	5	Ernie T. Poulos	Jeffrey Sullivan	IRE
1992	Pleasant Tap	5	Christopher Speckert	Buckland Farm	VA
1993	Bertrando	4	Robert J. Frankel	Ed Nahem and Marshall Naify	CA
1994	The Wicked North	5	David Bernstein	Philip & Sophie Hersh Trust	KY
1995	Cigar	5	William I. Mott	Allen E. Paulson	MD
1996	Cigar	6	William I. Mott	Allen E. Paulson	MD
1997	Skip Away	4	Sonny Hine	Carolyn Hine	FL
1998	Skip Away	5	Sonny Hine	Carolyn Hine	FL
1999	Victory Gallop	4	W. Elliott Walden	Prestonwood Farm	CAN
2000	Lemon Drop Kid	4	Scotty Schulhofer	Jeanne G. Vance	KY
2001	Tiznow	4	Jay M. Robbins	Cee's Stable	CA
2002	Left Bank	5	Todd A. Pletcher	Michael B. Tabor	KY
2003	Mineshaft	4	Neil J. Howard	W.S. Farish/W.T. Webber/J. Elkins	KY
2004	Ghostzapper	4	Robert J. Frankel	Frank Stronach	KY
2005	Saint Liam	5	Richard E. Dutrow Jr.	M/M William K. Warren Jr.	KY
2006	Invasor	4	Kieran McLaughlin	Shadwell Stable	ARG
2007	Lawyer Ron	4	Todd A. Pletcher	Stonewall Farm	KY
2008	Curlin	4	Steve Asmussen	Stonestreet Stables/ Midnight City Stables	KY
2009	Gio Ponti	4	Christophe Clement	Castleton Lyons	KY
2010	Blame	4	Albert M. Stall Jr.	Claiborne Farm	KY
2011	Acclamation	5	Donald Warren	Old English Rancho	CA
2012	Wise Dan	5	Charles Lopresti	Morton Fink	KY
2013	Wise Dan	6	Charles Lopresti	Morton Fink	KY

NOTES

PREFACE

1. Heller, *Forego.*

CHAPTER 1

2. Resnick, *Always a Fan*, 151.
3. The game, though not called by this name, was played in the fourteenth-century book *Piers Plowman*.
4. Ron Amundson, http://www.uhh.hawaii.edu/~ronald/HandicapDefinition.htm.
5. Ryan Goldberg, "Big Weights a Thing of the Past," *Daily Racing Form*, October 21, 2009.
6. Gary West, "Carry That Weight," *Blood-Horse*, March 5, 2003.
7. Goldberg, "Big Weights a Thing of the Past."
8. McCanliss, *Weight on the Thoroughbred Racehorse*, 279.
9. Ibid.
10. Ibid.
11. Thoroughbred Heritage, "Surrey-Epsom," http://www.tbheritage.com/TurfHallmarks/Gazeteer/GazeteerSurrey.html.
12. Annie Johnson, "The First Kentucky Derby—Unhorsed by the Louisville Cup?" *Antebellum Turf Times*, April 28, 2013.

13. Gatto, *Churchill Downs.*
14. McCanliss, *Weight on the Thoroughbred Racehorse*, 285.
15. The Brooklyn Handicap was not held in 1911 or 1912 due to New York's ban on parimutuel betting.
16. The Manhattan Handicap was run on dirt in 1977, 1979 and 1988.

CHAPTER 2

17. Daily Racing Form, *Champions*, 36.
18. Hollingsworth, *The Great Ones*, 226.
19. Neil Newman, "Roseben: Weight Could Slow Him, But He Won Under 147 pounds." *Blood-Horse*, February 21, 1948, 540.
20. Hollingsworth, *The Great Ones*, 227.
21. Ibid.
22. Carter and Kane, *150 Years of Racing in Saratoga.*
23. Daily Racing Form, *Champions*, 36.
24. Newman, "Roseben," 542.
25. *New York Times*, "Roseben Won at a Mile Galloping in Front: Sprinter Beat Rams Horn as He Pleased for Sterling Stakes," April 26, 1906.
26. Ibid., 225.
27. Newman, "Roseben," 542.
28. Hollingsworth, *The Great Ones*, 225.
29. Newman, "Roseben," 542.
30. Hollingsworth, *The Great Ones*, 226.
31. Ibid., 225–26.
32. The record was broken by Honeymoon in the Sequoia Handicap in 1946 (renamed the A Gleam Handicap in 1979) in a time of 1:20:40. Bold Ruler won the 1956 Vosburgh Handicap in 1:21 2/5 by nine lengths.
33. *Daily Racing Form*, October 16, 1905.
34. Hollingsworth, *The Great Ones*, 226.
35. *New York Times*, "Roseben Top Weight; Champion Sprinter Has Post of Honor for Carter Handicap," March 21, 1907.
36. *Montreal Gazette*, "Roseben Favorite," April 15, 1907.
37. *New York Times*, "Roseben, Champion Sprinter, Is Dying," September 20, 1907.
38. Hollingsworth, *The Great Ones*, 227.
39. Newman reports $74,910 in "Roseben," 543.
40. *Thoroughbred Record*, April 1911, cited at http://voices.yahoo.com/roseben-big-train-champion-racehorse-set-records-381302.html.

CHAPTER 3

41. *American Racing Manual, 1914*, cited in Hollingsworth, *The Great Ones*, 221.
42. Ibid.
43. Ibid., 222.
44. Ibid., 221.
45. Daily Racing Form, *Champions*, 34.
46. *New York Times*, "Old Roamer Wins Saratoga Handicap for the Third Time and Breaks Track Record," August 1, 1918.
47. Hotaling, *They're Off!* 202.
48. Ibid.; Ours, *Man o' War*, 158.
49. http://www.spiletta.com/UTHOF/roamer.html.
50. Hollingsworth, *The Great Ones*, 223.
51. Interview originally published in the *Daily Racing Form* and reprinted in the *British Bloodstock Breeders' Review* 7, no. 4 (December 1918): 367. See also http://www.brisnet.com/cgi-bin/static.cgi?page=historical_cameos_11.

CHAPTER 4

52. Blood-Horse Publications, *Horse Racing's Top 100 Moments*, 107.
53. Eva Jolene Boyd, "Exterminator," *The Backstretch*, July/August, 1999, 113.
54. Ennor and Mooney, *World Encyclopedia of Horse Racing*, 118.
55. Boyd, *Exterminator*.
56. Ibid.
57. The purchase price is subject to extensive speculation. McDaniel quoted this amount, according to Boyd, *Exterminator*.
58. Ibid.
59. Ibid.
60. Ibid.
61. http://www.spiletta.com/UTHOF/exterminator.html.
62. *New York Times*, "Man o' War and Exterminator win Feature Stakes on Final Days of Saratoga Racing," August 31, 1919.
63. Neil Newman, "Exterminator: His Steadiness Made Him America's Favorite," *Blood-Horse*, November 27, 1948, 558.
64. *Binghamton Press*, "Exterminator Sets American Running Record for Two Miles," September 16, 1920.
65. *New York Times*, "Exterminator Wins Toronto Autumn Cup in Close Finish," September 26, 1920.

66. Ibid., "Pimlico Cup Won by Exterminator," *New York Times*, November 13, 1921.
67. Ibid.
68. To date, this is the most weight ever carried by the winner in this race.
69. *New York Times*, "Exterminator Wins Brooklyn Handicap," June 17, 1922.
70. Neil Newman, "Exterminator," 562.
71. Ibid.
72. *Blood-Horse*, "The Exterminator Saga Ends," October 6, 1945, 581.

CHAPTER 5

73. *Thoroughbred Record*, "Death Comes to Equipoise," August 6, 1938, 103.
74. Philip Ardery, "The Chocolate Soldier," *Spur*, September/October 1984, 54.
75. www.spiletta.com/UTHOF/equipoise.html.
76. Equipoise was disqualified from first place in the Youthful.
77. www.spiletta.com/UTHOF/equipoise.html.
78. Ibid.
79. Ibid.
80. Ardery, "The Chocolate Soldier," 54.
81. Whitney, *High Peaks*, 33–34.
82. Ardery, "The Chocolate Soldier," 55.
83. Ibid.
84. Ibid.
85. Ibid.
86. Whitney, *High Peaks*, 38.
87. Daily Racing Form, *Champions*, 57.
88. Ardery, "The Chocolate Soldier," 57.
89. Ibid.
90. Ibid.
91. The race was run as the Equipoise Handicap in 1964–65 and from 1968 to 1997. It was hosted by Washington Park from 1943 to 1945 and was not in the years 1970–78, 1988, 1998 and 1999.

CHAPTER 6

92. Hollingsworth, *The Great Ones,* 89
93. www.spiletta.com/UTHOF/discovery.html.
94. Hollingsworth, *The Great Ones*, 89.
95. Ibid.
96. Ibid.
97. Tom McCormack, "Discovery: The Standard By Which Weight Carriers Are Judged," *Horse Racing* 1, no. 5 (August 1991): 10.
98. *New York Times*, "Discovery Victor; Clips World Mark; 40,000 at Narragansett See Colt Run Mile and Three-Sixteenths in 1:55," September 3, 1934.
99. Hollingsworth, *The Great Ones*, 90.
100. Ennor and Mooney, *World Encyclopedia of Horse Racing,* 116.
101. *New York Times*, "25,000 See Discovery Win," August 10, 1935.
102. Hollingsworth, *The Great Ones*, 91.
103. Bryan Field, "15,000 Watch Spa Racing," *New York Times*, August 22, 1936.
104. Hollingsworth, *The Great Ones,* 91.

CHAPTER 7

105. Palmer, *American Race Horses 1944*, 45.
106. Hervey, *American Race Horses 1941*, 53.
107. Ibid.
108. Daily Racing Form, *Champions*, 96.
109. Prior to 1989, the race was run as part of Keeneland's spring meeting. Since that time, it has been run in October.
110. *Prescott Evening Courier*, "Devil Diver Has Promise," April 10, 1942.
111. Palmer, *American Race Horses 1944,* 46.
112. Daily Racing Form, *Champions*, 94.
113. Ibid.
114. *Sportsman Review*, "Belmont Opens Spring Racing," May 11, 1943.
115. Hervey and Dunstan, *American Race Horses 1943*, 42.
116. Ibid., 42–43.
117. *Montreal Gazette*, "Devil Diver Beats Marriage by Nose," June 14, 1943.
118. *St. Petersburg Times*, "Devil Diver Upset Winner in Brooklyn," June 27, 1943.
119. Palmer, *American Race Horses 1945*, 28. Banastar also won all three but in different years.

120. Hervey and Dunstan, *American Race Horses 1943*, 45.
121. Palmer, *American Race Horses 1944*, 45.
122. *Sarasota Herald-Tribune*, "Devil Diver Wins Metropolitan Mile," May 14, 1944.
123. Palmer, *American Race Horses 1944*, 27.
124. *Lewiston Daily Sun*, "Arcaro on Devil Diver Wins Whitney," August 16, 1944.
125. Palmer, *American Race Horses 1944*, 48.
126. Duke, *Women of the Year.*
127. *Milwaukee Journal*, "Devil Diver Wins Belmont Feature," June 17, 1945.
128. Palmer, *American Race Horses 1944*, 47.

CHAPTER 8

129. Daily Racing Form, *American Racing Manual 1952*, 51.
130. Daily Racing Form, *American Racing Manual 1954*, 45.
131. Stone, *Belmont Park*, 54.
132. http://horseracinghalloffame.com/2002/12/15/ted-atkinson/.
133. Jason Diamos, "Ted Atkinson, Hall of Fame Jockey for Tom Fool, Dies at 88," *New York Times*, May 7, 2005.
134. http://www.spiletta.com/UTHOF/tomfool.html.
135. Palmer, *American Race Horses 1951*, 124.
136. *Blood-Horse*, "Death of Tom Fool," August 30, 1976.
137. http://www.spiletta.com/UTHOF/tomfool.html.
138. Dan Farley, "Tom Fool," *Thoroughbred Record*, August 28, 1976, 204.
139. http://www.spiletta.com/UTHOF/tomfool.html.
140. Estes, *American Race Horses 1952*, 93.
141. Daily Racing Form, *Champions*, 173.
142. Estes, *American Race Horses 1952*, 94.
143. Farley, "Tom Fool," *Thoroughbred Record* 204, August 28, 1976.
144. *Blood-Horse*, "Death of Tom Fool," August 30, 1976, 3,713.
145. Eclipse Press, *Horse Racing's Top 100 Moments*, 52.
146. http://www.spiletta.com/UTHOF/tomfool.html.
147. Ibid.
148. Estes, *American Race Horses 1953*, 54.
149. Daily Racing Form, *The American Racing Manual, 1954.*
150. *Blood-Horse*, "Death of Tom Fool," August 30, 1976, 3,714.
151. Ibid.
152. The August 30, 1976 *Blood-Horse* reports thirty shares at $50,000 each.

153. Farley, "Tom Fool," *Thoroughbred Record* 204, August 28, 1976, 765.
154. Jimmy Jamail, "The Question: Which Is, or Was, the Greatest Race Horse You Have Ever Ridden? (Asked of 10 Top American Jockeys)," *Sports Illustrated*, July 29, 1957.

CHAPTER 9

155. Joe Hirsch quoted in Haskin, *Kelso.*
156. http://www.spiletta.com/UTHOF/kelso.html.
157. Scatoni, *Finished Lines.*
158. Reeves, *Belmont Park*, 76.
159. Blood-Horse Publications, *Thoroughbred Champions*, 22.
160. http://www.racingmuseum.org/hall-of-fame/horse-trainers-view.asp?varID=85.
161. *Boston Globe*, "Carl Hanford, 95; Trained Thoroughbred Great Kelso," August 24, 2011.
162. Blood-Horse Publications, *Thoroughbred Champions*, 22–23.
163. Gatto, *Belmont Park.*
164. Ennor and Mooney, *World Encyclopedia of Horse Racing.*
165. Blood-Horse Publications, *Thoroughbred Champions*, 23.
166. Hollingsworth, *The Great Ones*, 157.
167. Gatto, *Belmont Park.*
168. http://www.spiletta.com/UTHOF/kelso.html
169. Hollingsworth, *The Great Ones*, 158.
170. Whitney Tower, "Move Over, Man o' War," *Sports Illustrated*, November 11, 1963.
171. Ennor and Mooney, *World Encyclopedia of Horse Racing.*
172. Blood-Horse Publications, *Thoroughbred Champions*, 24.
173. Joe Nichols, "Kelso a Horse for the Ages," *New York Times*, October 31, 1964.
174. *Blood-Horse*, March 19, 1966.

CHAPTER 10

175. *Thoroughbred Record*, "Damascus: Heart of Steel," March 22, 1986, 1,558.
176. Heckman, *Damascus.*
177. http://www.spiletta.com/UTHOF/damascus.html.
178. Heckman, *Damascus.*

179. Whiteley was quoted in a *Morning Telegraph* interview; Ibid.
180. Daily Racing Form, *Champions*, 202.
181. *Blood-Horse*, "Hot Times: The Rivalry of Dr. Fager and Damascus Turns 40," March 10, 2007, 1,446.
182. Shoemaker, *Shoemaker*, 109–10.
183. *Thoroughbred Record*, "Damascus: Heart of Steel," March 22, 1986, 1561.
184. *Palm Beach Post*, "Damascus Breaks Loose for Stakes Win at Aqueduct," September 5, 1967.
185. Blood-Horse Publications, *Horse Racing's Top 100 Moments*, 127.
186. Whitney Tower, "Damascus by a Mile," *Sports Illustrated*, October 9, 1967.
187. Secretariat earned $860,404 for his three-year-old season.
188. Hatton, *American Racing Manual 1967.*
189. *Daily News*, "Damascus Wins Brooklyn in Record Time," July 19, 1968.
190. Ibid.

CHAPTER 11

191. Blood-Horse Publications, *Thoroughbred Champions*, 38.
192. Heller, *Forego.*
193. Ibid.
194. Steve Haskin, "The Mighty Forego," *Blood-Horse*, June 21, 2009.
195. Heller, *Forego.*
196. Ibid.
197. Ibid.
198. William Leggett, "Forego Makes It Foregone," *Sports Illustrated*, October 6, 1975.
199. Ibid.
200. William Leggett, "A Race He Should Have Foregone," *Sports Illustrated*, August 15, 1977.
201. Heller, *Forego.*
202. Ibid.
203. Ibid.
204. Ibid.
205. Ibid.
206. Blood-Horse Publications, *Thoroughbred Champions*, 40. Exterminator carried 134 pounds in the Ontario Jockey Club Cup at Woodbine at a distance of two and a quarter miles on October 2, 1920.
207. Heller, *Forego.*

208. Ibid.
209. Ibid.
210. William Leggett, "An Opinion That Carries Much Weight," *Sports Illustrated*, October 11, 1976.
211. Toledo Blade, "Great Contractor Victor, Forego Vanquished," July 24, 1977.
212. William Leggett, "A Race He Should Have Foregone."
213. Haskin, "The Mighty Forego."

CHAPTER 12

214. Palmer, *American Race Horses 1945*, 27.
215. Whitney Tower, "Mr. Handicapper," *Sports Illustrated*, June 11, 1956.
216. Ibid.
217. Goldberg, "Big Weights a Thing of the Past."
218. Ibid.
219. Gary West, "Carry That Weight."
220. Sherry Ross, "Unshaded to Throw Weight Around in Whitney, Albert Has Great Burden," *NY Daily News*, July 27, 2001.
221. Ibid.
222. Kent Hollingsworth, "Handicaps Are Back, But as Lightweights," *Racing Times*, January 18, 1992.
223. Goldberg, "Big Weights a Thing of the Past."
224. Ibid.
225. Jack Shinar, "Wise Dan Handles Test in Fourstardave Repeat," *Blood-Horse*, August 10, 2013.

Sources

Blood-Horse Publications. *Horse Racing's Top 100 Moments*. Lexington, KY: Eclipse Press, 2006.

———. *Thoroughbred Champions: Top 100 Racehorses of the 20th Century*. Lexington, KY: Eclipse Press, 1999.

Boyd, Eva Jolene. *Exterminator*. Lexington, KY: Eclipse Press, 2002.

Carter, Allan, and Mike Kane. *150 Years of Racing in Saratoga: Little-Known Stories and Facts from America's Most Historic Racing City*. Charleston, SC: The History Press, 2013.

Daily Racing Form. *The American Racing Manual 1952*. New York: Daily Racing Form, 1953.

———. *The American Racing Manual 1954*. New York: Daily Racing Form, 1955.

———. *The American Racing Manual 1967*. New York: Daily Racing Form, 1967.

———. *Champions: The Lives, Times, and Past Performances of America's Greatest Thoroughbreds*. New York: Daily Racing Form, 2005.

Duke, Jacqueline. *Women of the Year: Ten Fillies Who Achieved Horse Racing's Highest Honor*. Lexington, KY: Eclipse Press, 2004.

Ennor, George, and Bill Mooney. *The World Encyclopedia of Horse Racing*. London: Carlton Books, 2001.

Estes, Joe A. *American Race Horses 1952*. New York: A.S. Barnes & Co., 1953.

———. *American Race Horses 1953*. New York: A.S. Barnes & Co., 1954.

Gatto, Kimberly. *Belmont Park*. Charleston, SC: The History Press, 2013.

———. *Churchill Downs*. Charleston, SC: The History Press, 2010.

Haskin, Steve. *Kelso*. Lexington, KY: Eclipse Press, 2003.

Hatton, Charles. *American Racing Manual 1967*. Daily Racing Form, 1968.

Heckman, Lucy. *Damascus*. Lexington, KY: Eclipse Press, 2004.

Heller, Bill. *Forego*. Lexington, KY: Eclipse Press, 2000.

Hervey, John. *American Race Horses 1941*. N.p.: Sagamore Press, 1942.

Hervey, John, and Nelson Dunstan. *American Race Horses 1943*. N.p.: Sagamore Press, 1944.

Hollingsworth, Kent. *The Great Ones*. Lexington, KY: Blood-Horse Publications, 1970.

Hotaling, Edward. *They're Off! Racing at Saratoga*. New York: Syracuse University Press, 1995.

McCanliss, Irene. *Weight on the Thoroughbred Racehorse*. Privately printed, 1967.

Ours, Dorothy. *Man o' War: A Legend Like Lightning*. New York: St. Martin's Press, 2006.

Palmer, Joe H. *American Race Horses 1944*. N.p.: Sagamore Press, 1946.

———. *American Race Horses 1945*. N.p.: Sagamore Press, 1946.

———. *American Race Horses 1951*. New York: A.S. Barnes & Co., 1952.

Resnick, Mike. *Always a Fan*. Rockville, MD: Wildside Press, 2009.

Scatoni, Frank. *Finished Lines: A Collection of Memorable Writings on Thoroughbred Racing*. New York: Daily Racing Form Press, 2002.

Shoemaker, Bill. *Shoemaker: America's Greatest Jockey*. New York: Doubleday, 1988.

Stone, Richard. *Belmont Park: A Century of Champions*. Lexington, KY: Eclipse Press, 2005.

Whitney, C.V. *High Peaks*. Lexington: University Press of Kentucky, 1977.

PERIODICALS

Antebellum Turf Times
The Backstretch
Binghamton Press
Blood-Horse
Boston Globe
British Bloodstock Breeders Review
Daily News
Daily Racing Form
Horse Racing
Lewiston Times
Milwaukee Journal
Montreal Gazette
New York Daily News
New York Times
Palm Beach Post
Prescott Evening Courier
Racing Times
Sarasota Herald-Tribune
Sports Illustrated
The Sportsman Review

The Spur
St. Petersburg Times
The Thoroughbred Record
Toledo Blade

INDEX

W

X

Z

About the Author

Melanie Greene is a doctoral candidate in the Faculty of Education at Memorial University of Newfoundland. She has published numerous articles in peer-reviewed academic journals. She holds a BA and MA in sociology and has completed programs in equine studies at the University of Guelph. Melanie has been an avid equestrian for much of her life. She has competed in dressage and hunter jumper divisions in her local horse community, as well as with the McMaster University Equestrian Team in Hamilton, Ontario. Melanie is the author of one other book, *Nasrullah: Forgotten Patriarch of the American Thoroughbred*. She currently resides in her hometown of St. John's, Newfoundland.